MW01167488

AMBITIOUS HEROES

AND

HEARTACHE

A BOOK ABOUT WHAT IT MEANS TO BE HUMAN

BY

RICK ALEXANDER

ISBN: 978-1-09830-032-6 (softcover)
ISBN: 978-1-0983-0033-3 (eBook)

This book is dedicated to a more complex understanding of the human experience. Through understanding, we gain perspective. Through perspective, we find the path that is apt to change our lives.

Table of Contents

Chapter 1

WHAT IF IT'S
THE WRONG DRAGON?

"Sometimes you go fight a dragon and it eats you.
And if you being eaten wasn't a real possibility
then it wouldn't be a real fight."

— Jordan Peterson

As children, most of us assume that by the time we grow up and become adults, we will have life all figured out. At a minimum, we tend to believe that we will at least have ourselves figured out. We are exposed to books and stories that bombard our imaginations with epic tales of kings that step into their glory, underdogs that win against the odds, and improbable romances that despite the struggle, always seem to find their way back to a happy ending. We are indoctrinated into an axiomatic life that's been modeled off of the blueprint that all of humanity has collectively left us. The story you know is the collection of many stories that have been distilled down through time and passed on to you.

Tragedy is almost always left to the antagonist of the stories we watch, which we have all concluded and agreed is exactly what should happen. Throughout the unfolding of the story, in our minds eye we automatically see ourselves in the reflection of the story's hero. Since we always assume that we are personally in alignment with what is right in the world, we conclude that the bad guy deserved whatever fate he received. The fact that it's entirely possible that our own actions cast us as the bad guy in our own stories (by our own definition of good and bad) is an afterthought that rarely makes its way inside of our awareness. By the time the story wraps up, we are so captivated by it, in part because we have mentally reserved the "ride off into the sunset" for ourselves. The story always ends when the hero slays the dragon (metaphorically or physically) and rescues the girl.

The movies always seem to cut scene before the hero starts to realize he isn't particularly happy with the girl or the relationship. Or when the girl realizes that her prince was good at slaying dragons, but personally they have different love languages and as a result haven't had a meaningful connection in years. It won't be long before both start to question why they even slayed the dragon in the first place. "How did we get here?" they'll wonder as they struggle to rekindle the fire that was once between them.

Maybe it was the wrong dragon? Maybe they're with the wrong person? Maybe it's the wrong life altogether? What does life look like after that kind of excitement ends? Surely there is some post-traumatic stress disorder (PTSD) involved? At a minimum, there has to be a huge emotional let-down to deal with once the couple realizes that life is pretty monotonous after the dragon has already been slain. As the passionate adventure that once fueled their connection becomes a distant memory, it is likely that their remaining connection will fade as well.

For those of us that have hit the hallowed halls of adulthood only to find ourselves entrenched in the monotony of our lives, we have a habit of growing cynical as the life we've put our hope into isn't matching up with the reality we are experiencing. The cynicism is not from the actual reality as much as it is from the frustration of knowing what it could be, or holding onto an idea about what it's supposed to be. After a few decades on Earth, we begin to feel like we've been sold a bill of goods. We accepted a no-money-down guarantee that promised fairy tales and movies, but were left with the tab as we shoulder disappointments and unimaginable heartache.

There is always an element of embellishment over time, as the stories we tell tend to become legend and take on a transcendent nature making them larger than life. However, it is important to understand that all stories start out with a human who was just moving through her life, doing the best that she can. She was a rejected, disappointed, confused, angry, happy, grateful, loving person just trying to figure it all out. Just like you are.

People overlook the fact that for most of his life, King Arthur was just Arthur. He was a peasant struggling to find his way in the world. Even when he found his path, he shouldered unimaginable imposter syndrome as he struggled to step into the glory of his birthright. If we are going to compare ourselves to what we've seen, we at least have to talk about the part of the story we are never told.

The role of stories in our life is never ending. On an individual level, we add stories to everything in our lives that we personally experience. This is our internal narrative and it's how we make sense of our world. Everything you do or don't do is the result of a story about that thing which you have conceptualized in your mind, and continue to tell yourself. How you feel about your life in general is typically the result of your mini-stories working into your overarching story, and how well you feel that those fit together. This will be referenced as cohearence.

When things go drastically wrong in life, the thing that hurts isn't always what went wrong, but the fact that our world no longer makes any sense or matches up to what we had hoped. When we feel ourselves slipping into chaos, it's because reality is constantly serving up error messages. It's telling us that we've mapped the world out incorrectly. In this case we are presented with a choice; find a new narrative that accounts for what went wrong or stay stuck. Those are the only two options because without cohearence, humans don't have an ability to move forward. Our narratives create our brains map for navigating the world. Consider the fact that it's almost impossible to get anywhere you want to go when you are in a place you don't understand and your map doesn't match the geography presented.

The stories and tales we tell in legend actually happened in one form or another, and the truth within them is deeper than the climate of our current society. In fact, humans developed the ability to tell a story because that is how we inherit collected wisdom. Due to the fact that we live for such a short period of time, it helps us understand ourselves better on a very fundamental level. The rhythm built into a story arch is the rhythm we've observed playing itself out through humanities countless efforts to forge ahead valiantly despite all that we find ourselves up against. We have learned to succeed despite the odds and the frailty of our condition. Stories about legends are stories about you. The disconnection in your own life isn't because reality is a disappointment, it's because we aren't taught to be legends.

Chapter 2

REFRAMING THE FALLOUT

"Some things benefit from shocks; they thrive and grow when exposed to volatility, randomness, disorder, and stressors and love adventure, risk, and uncertainty."

— Nassim Nicholas Taleb,
Antifragile: Things That Gain From Disorder

The thing to know about people who slay dragons is that far too often they define themselves by the dragons they conquer. By doing this, they inadvertently plant their flag in the past. The thing to know about yourself is that as soon as you connect who you are to a specific thing or achievement, every subsequent day that passes can only bring you further from the identity that you have manufactured. Due to the fact that time moves forward and material is static, you will inevitably find that you have chosen to define yourself by something that no longer exists, except in your mind. As a general rule, whenever you are operating in past thoughts, you are no longer operating in reality.

Your true self is present right here and now. Anything that isn't contingent on the moment is a fabrication of what is real. Any other identity can only be a false identity because whoever you are is here now, in a new moment doing something new. Who you truly are is the one that moves through time, evolving from moment to moment. You are not your job, your relationships, your accomplishment or your perceived failings; you are the one that experiences these things as you evolve through time.

For most of us, the thought of an identity that is not rooted in something solid brings infinite anxiety. We are used to being able to tell people who we are in material terms. The problem is, who you are is far beyond the material. You are not the momentary achievement that occurs at this stage in your life because the next stage is right around the corner. We struggle to hold the lies of our identity together, because we rarely understand that they are a lie. A more fluid view of ourselves is more consistent with what's actually true. As you can imagine, part of you is really struggling to hold it all together and you are getting utterly burned out as you continuously defend an identity that no longer exists.

As far as our hero and our princess go from chapter one, their entire identities were wrapped up in their adventure and the pursuit. As a result of the post-adventure waning excitement, they are both going to be feeling quite empty. They will probably try to rekindle the flame by doing what they used to do. Most likely that will consist of trying to relive some of the glory days that had while falling in love in the first place. Unfortunately, time and evolution are similar in that they only move in one direction in this life. Both parties will feel the inauthenticity at a visceral level. True connection can only be built on what is real in the moment.

This knowledge gives us an interesting opportunity. You can always choose to evolve with time, which is the natural state of everything that is alive and thriving. You can just as easily choose to cling to what's been comfortable and stay sedentary, which is the natural state of everything that finds itself in decay in this life. Trying to go backwards doesn't serve to restore the good times, only to serve as a cheap imitation that no longer fulfills you. For the record, there are glory days, but they are happening now.

As the couple's identity is swept further from the present moment by the tides of time, they will eventually begin looking for new things to fill the void they feel in their identities only to realize that they really don't know who they are anymore. Eventually, there won't be enough things or adventures to keep them preoccupied from the truth. One of them may come up with the idea to have children or move to a new town in order to rekindle love but as long as they believe that love requires a stimulus or exists as someplace to arrive outside of themselves, the result will be the same. They will end up apart, wondering what in the hell the whole thing was for in the first place. More often than not, that's the reality that life serves up.

We watch movies about the hero's journey because they do a "cut scene." They make us feel optimistic about the future because it appears that things work out. You and I however, have to exist here in the real world long after the credits end. It is important to remember that while these stories come to an end, real life doesn't. When stories end, we don't. We interpret stories as if there is a finality to them and the sunset is a place to finally "arrive." We treat our lives the same way, searching for our proverbial sunset, postponing our happiness and contentment until we find it.

The implications of this is that we attach the wrong success metrics to each part of our own story. For example, we identify the fact that there is somewhere to "arrive," and then, everything we do gets put through a lens that makes us believe that if we don't get there, we have failed. A predominant narrative put forth by our society is that if a romantic relationship doesn't result in marriage, and then that marriage doesn't last forever, we should look at that relationship as a failure. We then further look at that failure as a waste of time and we wonder why we wasted so much our time on that person. If "forever" is the standard of success in a world of total impermanence, we have the unfortunate habit of putting ourselves into games that we can't win.

The inherent problem with this view is that it doesn't leave room for growth or evolution, let alone enjoyment. If the path of two people's lives came together in a world of impermanence and chaos, and they are able to share something as sacred as love, the highest expression of our humanity, it is wildly inaccurate to consider that a waste of time. You are always learning more about what you want and don't want, setting you up for an even better future. Plus, you get to experience incredible pleasure periodically throughout the lesson. A little gratitude for what you've gone through will go a long way in helping you make sense of your life. Understand that stories are seasons, and you will live through many of those seasons in this one life alone. If you learn from each lesson along the way, the seasons have this incredible quality of getting better.

Appreciating the beauty and magnitude of the world we live in is largely due to how we frame it. Gratitude has to remain at the root of everything we do if we want the frame to be productive for our mental, emotional, and spiritual health. Be thankful for every story, regardless of the perceived ending in this moment. It is likely that there is a much larger picture that is painted, and you are trying to judge it with the one myopic view of the brush stroke that you are currently taking in. Gratitude is how we remain grounded in humility when things are going well and it's how we remain hopeful when things are not. It gives us the perspective needed to accept our current invitation to live better.

If instead you look at everything you do here as a smaller part of a greater whole, then you are always succeeding. If you are open to it, experience is the best teacher that you will ever have. Everything we do in this life helps us to learn what we might do, in order to become who we might be. What if instead of arriving at an achievement, you put your focus on learning from the next step? What if this is all just an experience to learn lessons and evolve your soul in preparation for the eternal?

Positing such a theory might come off as far-fetched at first, but that's actually just the result of your current mindset and environmental setting. You haven't heard it before, so it stands out as improbable or absurd. When it comes to big philosophical ideas concerning the meaning of life, what's more improbable is the fact of existence itself. What's more absurd is that although none of us actually knows what happens when our hourglass runs out of sand, every culture seems to fall in love with their own theories about the beginning of the universe and then subsequently reject everyone else's. We don't look at our differences in theory as beautiful, but instead have seen them historically as something we should fight over.

In searching for what it really means to be human, what we need to prioritize is wisdom. When something is intelligent it is relatively true and cohearent for the environment it's presented in. When something is wise, it is eternally relevant. Wisdom can be found underlying every true capitulation of existence. It's what you get when you take the nuances out of every philosophy that's been passed through time from religion to stoic philosophy. This book is an attempt to distill wisdom, yet it should be noted that this requires a certain level of openness in order to attain.

There are billions of people on this planet, all originating from different cultures that have their own lens for looking at the world. It is unlikely that every origination story will work for every human. The fussing and fighting over the differences is often a result of childlike tendencies that we've brought with us into adulthood. We must remember that the footing of others says nothing about the validity of what you see from where you stand. Deep down, however, like scared children, we often feel insecure with our own beliefs and we try to strengthen our resolve by drawing lines in the sand. We often need to know that others are standing where we are, in order to quell our fears and so we are willing to fight with those who don't. This may be because we were never taught that it is okay to stand on our own and trust our own internal guidance system.

Despite these early naive beliefs about a storybook ending, the truth is that most of us lumber through life without any real intentions. We're taught from an early age what we should do, how we should act, and how to best assimilate into society in a way that is productive without causing too many waves. We are conditioned to believe that a successful life should look a certain way. Most of us do our best to emulate that idea. This is not the stuff of legends.

Under the surface of our ambitions, most of us have very little idea about who we really are or what we really want. We spend most of our lives trying to figure out what the world wants us to be. As a result, our own desires for our life are left peppered around the perceived responsibilities from which we were born. This is why most people live for the weekends. Monday through Friday we do what we "have to do." If there is any time left over, we "get" to do the things that make our souls come alive.

If we don't know what inspires us, that is, what breathes life into us, we are left with only those activities that dim the one part of our soul that is always trying to remind us that we are here for something more. The part of us that isn't so happy with our current lifestyle. Alcohol and other pacifiers don't just work because they help us cope with a less than stellar existence. They also help numb the part of us that won't tolerate that existence in the first place.

Thus, the world continues with its soul sucking jobs that monopolize our finite amount of time, while we are at the same time unknowingly propped up by industries of distraction. What does it say about the world we've constructed, when some of the biggest industries in it exist solely to help people cope with that world?

What's worse is that our culture has assigned an element of nobility into the model of giving the system our valuable time. This leaves most people with a feeling of shame if they do not conform to that model. The majority of people believe that they have to sacrifice who they really are and what they want in order to be of service to the people around them. If they first give to themselves what they need, they often feel selfish. It is important to remember - if you don't give yourself what you need, who will? Furthermore, are you actually serving the world as best you can if you aren't the best you can be? Can you be the best version of yourself if you perpetually don't get what you need? We should have the courage to ask ourselves and answer honestly; what serves the world more? The version of us that has all that it needs and finds passion in what it does or the version of us that subjugates itself to please others? Only one of these versions can give it's internal gifts to the world. The other is often far too exhausted to be of use outside of incessant people pleasing.

For some, even taking a single personal day in the middle of the work week creates a feeling of shame. This struggle indicates that you determine that your ability to be of service to the world around you is valuable only if you give up your own well-being. Why must we trade our joy for anything in a world that encapsulates everything? Surely we are not in a scenario that requires we forgo happiness for service. If you truly believe that and act it out, you have placed yourself in a scenario in which no one wins.

At most, this current disposition toward life is the leftover ideal of a society in which we no longer live. Whenever you find yourself in a situation in which you can't see a route out, it's because you have been participating in the wrong game. A solution always exists. That solution may just not exist within your current view of the world or within the story that you are telling yourself. A new point of view always reveals a new path out of chaos.

Chapter 3

THE SPIRIT OF ADVERSITY

"We are *Homo religiosu*, not in our desire for
creeds or constitution, nor in our commitments to
specific gods and theologies, but in our existential
striving toward transcendence: toward that which
lies beyond the manifest world."

— Reze Aslan

Humans experience consciousness at a level that appears to be higher
than everything else in the physical world. Our awareness has evolved so
widely that it encapsulates the knowledge of self. With this knowledge we
have come to understand that our depth isn't limited to only existing in the
physical world. As far as we know, humans are unlike other animals in this
way. We are uniquely aware of the fact that while we are finite (the "self"
that we can describe has borders as well as an expiration date), there are
aspects of our being which appear to exist in the infinite. While every culture has their own way of conceptualizing this transcendent nature, in their
own way, each of them use it as a form of guidance and strength for navigating the material world. Typically, this guidance comes as the result of an
inner knowing. In the gnostic and western mystic practices, this is known
as the divine spark. Eastern mysticism refers to it as "Brahman." In the

Abrahamic religions, it is expressed as, "being made in God's image." In new age spiritual endeavors, it is often referred to as the "higher self," or "true self." In this book, I'll refer to it often as "the soul" while laying out a case for it's unique importance in the human experience.

By the very nature of our being, some part of who we are has always been and always will be. According to the first law of thermodynamics, energy cannot be created nor destroyed. That means that some part of us, our soul, our essence, the energy that makes up the fabric of our existence, has always existed in one form or another. What that means for you and I is that we've literally waited billions of years to be in this very moment. My hope is that we start acting like it.

I've come to see that the energy that underlies our existence can be viewed in much the same way as the energy in the power grid. It's stored in the walls until one of us walks over and turns on a light switch. In that moment, the energy is then redistributed into the room as light where it is far more useful than it was while stored in the wires in the walls. When our energy is here in this form, and the switch is turned on, we can learn much about the characteristics of the soul by understanding the light.

Light doesn't have the desire to be validated or reciprocated, yet it's no less helpful. It doesn't need to know that its efforts are appreciated, yet it continues to guide those that need it. It doesn't matter how long something exists in the shadows; light will expose it without prejudice.

In identifying its qualities and characteristics, you gain the recognition that what is in the universe is also in you. It is through understanding the soul that we understand what unites each of us outside of form. Spirit and mystery exist without edges and so it is in that place that we can find unity with all living things.

As we engage further with life and we seek to explore how we might best conduct ourselves in this mysterious scenario, two things become evident. 1. The problems that we engage with in life actually end up defining our lives. 2. There is no way we could engage with our problems in a productive manner without the understanding that there is a right and a wrong way to do so. We define those as virtues and they serve as a north arrow for the human condition when we find ourselves lost in chaos. We recognize that something deep within us is ultimately aligned with those virtues. We retain the ability to recognize what is correct and align ourselves with it. This is why we all agree that if the protagonist in a story wins by what we consider to be cheating, we don't feel as though they've actually won. This is why *The Lion King* doesn't end with Scar ruling the kingdom. The spoils of prosperity are apparently reserved for those who take on their adversity in a forthright manner. That is the narrative that has been distilled through time. The light always prevails. In knowing this, we should each seek to foster our own.

Without this conception of an ultimate right and wrong, how would you know in which direction to move next? How would you know what the hero would do? Yet, regardless of the scenario that you find yourself in, you always have the ability to ask yourself what the hero would do if he or she were in your position. What you find in asking yourself this question is that you almost always know what that is. More often than not, our hesitation stems from realizing that what's right and what's difficult are one in the same.

We intrinsically find ourselves aligning with certain virtues that are presupposed to be in alignment with what is ultimately correct; be that God, gods, or a deeply ingrained human moral landscape. In any case, the stories that are told about the triumph of humanity have this north arrow built within them. These stories tell us that what is inside of us is ultimately true, and that we can look to that truth in times of trouble or tribulation.

Right before the climax of *The Lion King* story, Simba is wrestling with the idea of answering his calling and reclaiming the kingdom from Scar. Destiny often requires a level of responsibility that pushes many people to avoid the call, or to find the correct anesthetic that allows them to forget about it. Doing what we know to be right and living in our truth is a lot to take on. Otherwise, we wouldn't have so much trouble with it.

The pressures to do something else other than our calling are often far stronger than we recognize. We will spend all of our lives running errands, doing this thing or that, all the while avoiding the one thing that we know deep down we are here to do. Usually these distractions only serve the moment that they keep us occupied. If you find yourself within enough silence, all you must do is ask yourself "what is the one thing that you know that you need to do that you aren't doing?" The question you ask is a form of prayer and the answer, a form of divinity.

As Simba wrestles with the call, his attention is directed back toward the sky where his father (the conceptualization of God or the representation of what is right in the story, in this case, Mufasa) says to him, "Remember who you are." This is a nod toward his rightful place in the world. The path to this place always lies within us and we must only look there in order to find it. Whatever you find outside is normally only a distraction from the truth. *Hakuna Matata.*

The divine spark is the part of your essence or soul that is aligned with all that is good and right in the universe. It is the source of light and love and it is you just as much as the next human. It is what you must lean into when you find yourself trampling through the dark times that adversity has a way of pulling you into. This is why prolonged times of adversity or that iconic rock bottom moment are often referred to as the dark night of the soul. The benefit of rock bottom is that it usually does you the favor of stripping away everything that isn't important. When we relinquish the trivial things we're holding onto such as the need for validation, surface level relationships and material status, we find that's when the soul shines the brightest. This gives life to the phrase that the night is always darkest before the dawn.

Prior to the existence of the civilized world that we now know, many cultures required an individual to achieve a rite of passage to achieve adulthood. It was on this journey that we would often recognize our true calling in life. It was something like a forced rock bottom moment. The passage often required an extreme level of hardship, as this made it an extremely good filter for clarifying what matters to an individual. Clarifying what truly matters gives us direction because it syncs our direction to travel up with the desires of the soul. This is why the right answer is often felt just as much as it's intellectually known. Remember that when something is of the soul, it is an "inner knowing." This is manifested in our lives as a visceral feeling of peace with our direction.

When we don't have this feeling, we try to make decisions based on thought alone in order to navigate the world. When we only think about a solution, two things happen. 1. We tend to think in loops, meaning you'll never truly identify a way out of the loop. 2. We tend to prioritize what we can conceptualize, which are material metrics; the things we can measure and quantify. This is the kind of thing that pushes us to go to law school without ever really asking ourselves if practicing law sixty hours a week is what we truly want for our lives.

Our current culture exists without this passage and because of this, it is likely that most people won't figure out what they really want, or even who they really want to be, before their mid-thirties at a minimum. This is ironic, considering the fact that our culture also puts an untold amount of pressure on its citizens to stay on the path on which they currently travel. Many people are paralyzed by the prospect of pivoting careers or relationships in their thirties or forties. I feel blessed that my life fell apart when I was in my late twenties, so that I didn't have to spend another moment on a path that I was on simply because I thought it would make others appreciate me.

Currently, the closest thing that our culture has to rites of passage outside of the military (which requires an ideological alignment that doesn't work for everyone), is the university system. As of late, the university system is doing all that it can to erase hardship from the path. You see this with the censorship of speech and the prevalence of the infamous safe spaces. A safe space would be perfectly reasonable only if you have very little idea how humans develop themselves. A true rites of passage builds resilience because it is the only option presented in the face of overwhelming odds. Life has a way of presenting us with those odds whether we are ready for them or not.

We are simultaneously found and created on our path to become all that we can in this life. We find our spirit and resolve (our true selves) as we test our metal against the obstacles that require us to become the type of person that can overcome those types of obstacles. We are created in the same way that a blacksmith forges an iron weapon through repeated bouts of heat, hammering and twisting. In this way, so to do we become the sharpest and strongest version of ourselves as we are also exposed to such measures. This means that what we are really looking for in this life are the right obstacles that are going to require our adaptation. It is in that adaptation that our character and ultimately our legacy will be crafted.

Compare this to the metrics that most of us use to pick our path in life. "The benefits are good," "The job is stable," "The partner won't leave us." We can go on like this forever if we are not exposed to the right hardship and the subsequent relinquishing of what we thought mattered. Often, it is in this cycle of moving from one resume bullet to the next that we find the world begins to wear us out. The "grind" is aptly named as it inadvertently grinds down our resolve, our hope, and our imagination for what our lives could be. Somewhere in the midst of our grasp at material safety, we find that our spirit is slowly being extinguished.

The beautiful thing about the human experience is that the light within can never be fully extinguished. It may be covered under worry, people-pleasing, and whatever it is you've been told that you have to accept in this life. You and I both know, deep down, that you are meant for more. You have ideas about what your life could be and I'm here to tell you that there isn't a material metric or amount of safety in the world that could make avoiding that destiny actually worth it. All of the material in the world can only be a means to become who you ultimately want to be. When material is treated as an end, the stirring and questioning you feel from within is the soul's recognition that more still lies beyond the horizon.

Start down that path by understanding that the so-called problems in your life are inviting you to live differently today. Some people recognize problems in their life and begin to feel like it's just something else that is stacked against them. These problems are just something else holding them in place. The reality is that every problem you have in life is your invitation to live differently.

Learn to identify what angers you, when it doesn't serve you, and let it go. Learn to set boundaries from identifying what you resent. Learn that what you feel as injustice is a hint at underlying passion. It is the small voice within that will guide you to and through these things. The invitation is always present, waiting for us to step further into soul and transcending the pain that we cause with all of our taking and grasping and defining.

What you're truly looking for isn't the right job, person, or opportunity that lets you create the facade of safety; that's the state you create so that you jump from, not into. Humans require a level of psychological safety based on the proper order of things from which to explore the world. Without that, the entire thing just feels unsafe and we find ourselves constantly overwhelmed. This is the role of traditions, routines, and habits in our lives. We create these things to orient ourselves in time and space. Once we have a proper orientation, we are free to follow the path of the soul. The fact that the universe is always inviting us to live differently is often lost on us as we search our lives for the right opportunity. The truth is that we are always preparing to answer our call. Many of us will spend our lives chasing frivolous endeavors that we are told we "should" care about and each of these only serves to distract us from the true invitations that are directly in front of us.

The metrics that you use to judge the success of your endeavors will ultimately end up dictating the perspective through which you are looking. Understanding that is key to ensuring that you don't spend your life fighting the wrong dragon. A loss of a job for example, is only a truly bad thing if you allow that job to define you in some way. Perhaps it's actually just an invitation to live differently – to stop putting off what you actually want to be doing. The job of your soul is to evolve and so you might find that you are continuously putting yourself into situations that cause you to grow in an uncomfortable way. If you define success by the permanence of what you do, it is likely that you'll miss that lesson and perhaps, what is coming next. As you engage with various problems, you unlock certain potentiality that then opens up many doors.

Potential (another thing that exists beyond form, yet dictates the direction of our lives) is a never ending well. The more you engage with reality, the more that reality gifts you with the potential to do more. With every door that you walk through, what you find is a problem to solve that is only getting deeper. We're not moving along the horizon looking for challenges. We're actually digging for resources. As an example, you might not have the potential to run a marathon now but if you trained for a half marathon, it is likely that you would. Potential is given as the reward for engagement with life. Every problem gets a level deeper and you eventually end up moving closer to an ultimate problem. Something that will end up defining your life's work.

As humans, we have very selective attention and bandwidth. We get to pick small pieces of the universe and choose to make it better while we're here. Unfortunately, we are limited by our condition in our capacity to take on endeavors. It can be easy to get sucked into the "more is better" mentality and to begin believing that the key to a good life is somewhere between what we can amass and what we can accomplish. The truth is that all of those things are secondary. Those are outer purposes that exist beyond the evolution of your soul.

The belief system that many of us operate within is that we have to find our singular purpose in life. This is the trap of thinking there is a certain thing out there that will make you happy or complete once you find it. That thing is promised to you by anyone that wants your money and if you look around the world, people are willing to pay any price to get it. "The answer is out there somewhere and if you find it, you'll be complete." Typically, this promise is accompanied by a no money down guarantee that expires right before you reach it.

There is no real final destination outside of life itself. The truth is that you will have many different purposes throughout your time here on earth but the ultimate beauty is life itself. Beauty doesn't require validation outside of simple recognition. The universe is imperfectly perfect. What appears broken gives us something to strive against and explore. We have obstacles in which to test ourselves and become who we might and it's easy for us to get down on ourselves when we start trying to control an outcome instead of learning from the process.

The true nature of our lives is such that we are always being prepared for what is to come next. Many of us find that our lives are lived out in repeating cycles of the same scenarios with different faces and names because we never learn the current lesson for what's next. Instead of taking our invitation to evolve our soul, we stifle it's needs and continue to look for something else to make us feel complete. We date the same people, work the same jobs, and make the same mistakes, because we continue to play the wrong game. If your life is continuously serving you the same problem on repeat, you must only go within yourself to evolve your soul in that area and you will find that the problem leaves you. What internal dysfunction is causing you external pain?

What do you say that we just drop what we've known and experiment with another way to be? Maybe the depression rate and the obedience to metrics that aren't serving us any longer are just invitations from our cultures to live differently. Perhaps in this life there isn't somewhere to get after all. Maybe life is just an arena with built in trials and obstacles against which to wield ourselves. In this case, our goal would be to evolve the version of us that lies deeper than what we can see and what we can touch. Perhaps all we actually take with us when we leave this life is what we can become.

If you recognized this as true, would it change the way that you spent your time while you were here? Would your direction rely more on the divine spark that's present within? Would you listen to the voice that seems to emerge from that spark? Would you believe me if I told you that there was nowhere to actually get in life? That for all of your seriousness and your hustling and your endless doing, there isn't an arrival point that lets you keep one damn thing that you attain? Of course, you know this intellectually, but have you put thought into how that should affect your actions?

Chapter 4

THE SOUL'S KEEPER

"When the ego dies, the soul awakes."

— Mahatma Gandhi

Our current culture has produced a pattern. Endless people engage in endless hustle only to realize that the hand that is currently gripping all of their material will inevitably become the dirt that grows the trees, which will eventually be converted to money for someone else to grab. This is without exception. The greatest human hope is that we have the realization with time to act it out, before the conversion to dirt.

Given that this is the game that society has manufactured, the question becomes, how do we engage with it in a way that still leaves us room for contentment? If we still want to participate in the ongoing creation of the world around us, which most of us have a deep desire to do because we are after all, social animals, we must find the path that lies between the relinquishing of material held by the monks and the worship of material held by the ego. Since most people are uninterested in the former, we will focus on how to get what we want by transcending the latter.

At a fundamental level, your ego is a collection of thought patterns that have been formed in your mind about how you should be. It's helpful to think of it as a sub personality within yourself. The personality is created by patterned behavior and thought that has been ingrained so that you can navigate your way through the world. It's one of your deepest blue prints that tells you how to be in the world. Due to this, if you want to understand your ego better, you can start by looking at your first reactions to something. Your first thought often reflects your conditioning before your desires.

When someone cuts you off, it is your ego that pipes up next. When someone walks by you and their appearance isn't up to your standards, it is the voice of the ego that you hear in your head that is applying judgement to them. When you hear of a good opportunity to make money, it is your ego that wants to take said opportunity before seeing if it's in alignment with your value system or if you'll even be happy doing whatever it is that the opportunity has you doing. This last part is because the ego only understands where it is in the world based on hierarchies. One of the hierarchies that stand as the easiest for the ego to make sense of and climb is the one that is based on net worth. This is why we have so much trouble not allowing the above cycle to rule our lives. This also however, gives us a path to ego transcendence. If it is our first reaction that is conditioned by the ego, it is in our ability to pause and filter our thoughts and subsequent actions based on our knowledge which can begin to repattern the underlying conditioning.

As we age, we tend to find that we are stuck in the middle of many paradoxes and it is the feeling of being "stuck" between them that tends to force us into retreating for a more simple view of the world. We have an ego that is constantly reinforcing the fact that we are better than everyone around us (this is one of the ways that it assures itself that it is climbing the hierarchies). Our ego looks for subtle clues and build its case for why we are better than others. It is developed to various degrees for various people depending on how they were raised, but no one is exempt.

The paradox is found where you see that we also have a mind that evolved to find meaning in life and the ways that we actually derive lasting meaning are almost always running counter to the desires of the ego. To get true meaning we need connection while the ego will reinforce the

AMBITIOUS HEROES AND HEARTACHE

illusion of separation. To get true meaning we need passion and this often leads us to years of work on a craft or a sole mission that is aligned with who we are on a deep level. The ego is not interested in the long game and so you may notice that your first reaction is to find the route that is expedited.

The ego operates out of fear and obsesses on what it lacks so it will scan its environment and focus in on others that seem to be ahead of you. To the ego, what others have is a symbol of what you don't and so convinces itself that it must attain those things in order to feel whole. If you aren't careful it will also encourage you to take shortcuts to attain what they have. It wants to gain now and the easiest way to do that is usually with material. If the Joneses next door buy a new car, guess what the quickest way to level up the egoic hierarchy is?

The reason that "keeping up with the Joneses" is a saying in the first place is because so many people are familiar with the pull to put yourself ahead of your neighbor. We evolved to climb dominance hierarchies through nature and once that desire met self-awareness, we began to add a social element to our climbing. Now, it's not enough to feel like we are better than someone else but also, that others should know and recognize it. This is why the ego is so extremely magnified through the use of social media.

All of your life you will find that the desires of the ego appear to be at odds with what you want deep down. Those deep down desires are born of the soul. The ego sees the world as a zero sum game with only so many resources and opportunities and because of the fear that drives it, it must take to get and it must do it soon. You can always reason yourself into not truly going after what you want deep down, because the loudest voice you have is the ego and it will present lots of compelling evidence for getting what you need right now. "The money and the opportunities won't be there forever so you must seize them now. Later you can do what you really want once you are secure." This is another great lie of the ego because what's actually true is that money and opportunity will always exist. It's you that will not.

The soul, which is boundless outside of your body knows that you are here for more. It knows that opportunities are endless and that the world actually has far more than enough for all of us, if we would just start acting like it. The soul is passionate about things because it knows that you have a reason for being here. You have something to give or to do that is uniquely yours. Most likely, deep down, you know what this is. If you do not yet know, rest assured that your soul will give you nudges when it can no longer accept the parameters that the ego has put on it.

Through my work, I keep finding people who have the nudge, but have built their life down the path of the ego. At this time in our history, most humans are still living inside of their egos. People haven't yet "woken up" to the fact that life isn't about what and where you can get. This is why, if you ask for advice when you start feeling the nudge of the soul, most people won't encourage you to take some daring leap. Instead, you will be encouraged to stay the path. When leaving a previous job of twelve years because of my own soul's nudge, I couldn't believe how many unhappy people encouraged me to remain unhappy. What we do find is that if we want to pivot away from the empire (however big or small) that the ego has built, we run into some serious limits. We feel as though we are too invested in what we have done, we have gone too far or we have built too much status in order to leave. We tell ourselves we have come too far to start over. The moment when we decide to pivot is when we realize something incredible about our lives. The outer limits of our capabilities are defined by the space between our ears without exception. There are no rules to pivoting these days. There is nothing actually stopping you except about a thousand thoughts a day that tell you that you can't. We have always known this, but each person must come to find it in their own time. This is why, despite the path that you take to self realization through personal development, you will arrive back to the fact that the person that is standing in your way is actually just you.

If you are early on in the evolution of your thinking, it is likely that you haven't yet felt or at least acknowledged your soul's nudge. A lifetime of following the ego can make it extremely difficult to hear. Since our world is in the stage where the ego rules and has for years, the systems we have found are not very good at helping you develop your soul's path. For most people, the pivot away from the ego looks like them looking around in their own lives and realizing all of the material they've spent their lives emphasizing is providing them very little in terms of actual satisfaction.

When it comes to looking for advice, you will also run into far more born of the ego than soul due to sheer volume. You can hear the separate cries of the ego all through pop culture from music to television. You don't hear the soft voice of the soul as much because it often comes from monasteries, poets, and the still small voice within you (if you ever get quiet enough). The voices of ego are in your face everywhere you look because they are craving validation and material. If you follow these voices, you will validate and embolden them as well as your own. The wisdom that is encapsulated in the soul needs nothing from you, so you won't find it until you are ready.

Our systems have been developed to create people of industry. We have schools that train you to be factory workers in a world with fewer and fewer factories. We choose our professions, achievements, and even our relationships based off the conditioning that is ingrained within us early on. It leaves us feeling a bit disconnected from ourselves and our lives, to say the least. The demands of the world are now changing, but major systems will always be slow to change. If you zoom out far enough, you see that the world needed to be pushed by the ego in order for us to create the industrys that standardize the quality of lives for people on a massive level. As the world economy lifts more people out of poverty, you'll see a shift in collective consciousness. Remember that security and safety is where humans create from not into. As we become more secure and safe on a global scale, you will see more and more people heading toward self actualization since they will finally be free to do so.

Most people go through the motions quite successfully. They get the degree, they get the job, they get the mortgage, and they get the white picket fence. Most people master the things they "should" do. On the outside, all is well, so the cycle continues. What no one ever talks about is the dichotomy that is growing in the "successful" person's psyche when the achievements don't yield the fulfillment they thought they would. This is the internal questioning that we don't share. Why aren't I happy if I'm doing everything that I should? Am I not grateful for such an opportunity? So many others would kill to have this life, so why does it feel like it's eating me alive?

What many people find when they live their life as a "paint by numbers" is that there is the person that they are in the world, standing atop the dragons they've already slain for which everyone celebrates them. Then there is the silent yearning to be somewhere else, with someone else, doing something else. Navigating through that conditioning and bridging that disconnect can be overwhelming and trying, and that's just for people who actually do the thing they set out to do.

For millions more of us, we end up lost in our journey, mired in distress, and never really finding a direction for our efforts. When we find ourselves lacking intrinsic motivation as we chase the wrong dragon, the people around us eventually assume that we're lazy. What else could it be? When people don't fit in the exact system that we've set up, we tell them to be more like the people that do, we don't tell them to work on building a different system.

For most people, we've built up such internal walls around ourselves in order to keep us on the path that we believe we "should" be on, that the thought of stepping outside of the confines of what's expected brings too much fear, shame, and guilt to even consider it. Regardless of the fact that it's a crucial life skill, we're not all taught to improve our relationship with risk. This leaves us with an alarming shortage of tools for teaching ourselves to be happy and as a result, we find ourselves trapped by our own thinking. Since the ego has trouble standing on it's own, it will further push you to accept the metrics that the materially driven world is presenting. As a result, the world around us gets a watered down version of who we could be as the path we feel that we must accept but would not necessarily choose, rarely get our full efforts.

For the people who have to continually motivate themselves to go to the gym, or to work harder at their jobs, or to take care of the many responsibilities that they are told they should in life, the idea of pursuing their passions can sound unrealistic. How are people expected to find passion when they look around and feel nothing but apathy? What should they do when they look to pivot from that apathy and there is a society and an internal thought structure that tells them that where they are is where they are supposed to be?

Research consistently shows that in order for motivation to last, it must be intrinsic. In other words, the person has to want to move to actually move over the long term. Taking into account this defining characteristic of motivation, what you find aren't lazy people, but instead, people that actually just don't know themselves well enough to find a vision for their lives that actually pulls them forward. Instead, they are trying to push themselves based on standards that don't resonate with them. When this division exists inside of your psyche, forward progress becomes extremely difficult and contentment becomes impossible.

On the contrary, when you do find yourself living an authentic life, meaning that you are living somewhere that you want to live, pursuing work that is meaningful to you and associating with people that share your value system, than motivation, discipline, and the other qualities that are prized as success habits tend to become a byproduct of that life instead of something you have to constantly keep after yourself to achieve. This is difficult to understand if you've spent your life accepting less than you deserve. What you will find if you ever get on your true path is that you aren't lazy, dumb, or confused. Instead, you have just been incorrectly positioned for impact. We have an incredible opportunity to celebrate the uniqueness of the seven billion people that are on the planet today. Instead, the prevailing message by society that's corroborated by the ego is to subjugate whatever makes you different for the sake of fitting in. Most of us are simply never taught where to look for such things that will lead to intrinsic motivation. The world will present many options that seem palatable at first. The chances that you wind up down the wrong path are much greater than the chances that you wind up down the one that is truly right for you.

Throughout our lives, we are exposed to inputs that treat us more like a pinball, bouncing us around all of the different rules and expectations we are expected to adhere to, and be able to navigate. Then one day we turn eighteen and they tell us to start making decisions that will affect the rest of our lives. We take the list of "shoulds", "supposed tos", and expectations, and then we do our best to craft a life that we don't completely hate. We then find that we're strict on ourselves about how much we can pivot. At the risk of sounding crass, how could such a system lead to anything other than mass depression? With high hopes and a somewhat incomplete road map, we begin to throw ourselves into things prized by the ego, something we rarely understand, hoping that we will get to the happily ever after we grew up adoring on TV. With no real training about how to think about the things that we want in life, we often end up putting our hope on the whimsical intentions of the world around us. What we fail to recognize is that there is no final dragon and because of that, "happily ever after" isn't a destination but just an extension of the journey. One that you will have to continuously work to achieve and keep.

Over the years, we were taught what to do, but never how to think. The problem is that when what we should do doesn't yield the contentment that we were promised, we are out of options as the emphasis in our learning models today doesn't help us analyze the problem while taking in the full spectrum of what it means to be human. We have nuances and intricacies that need to be accounted for, and since the ego has a deep desire to fit in and not look different than others, we find that it desires to repress our nuances and act as if they don't exist.

The problem with repression is that it doesn't work. From a psychological standpoint, what happens is that the same urges end up being expressed, but in a way that you can't control. These expressions become known as shadows of our personality and are pushed outside of our awareness. Since our ego has decided that it doesn't want to be associated with them, it relinquishes control over them. When you don't deal with your shadows, you end up pulling the people around you into them, and you then become someone you don't like very much. Cue the self-loathing that we are all too familiar with. Outside of dealing with our shadows and integrating them into our personality, we are also never taught how to go about drawing our own conclusions about the many situations in which we will find ourselves, specifically when those situations deal with existential matters. We aren't given a frame work with how to process the metaphysical, the unexplainable, or the existential. In fact, it's quite the opposite.

We are told to never discuss religion, money, or politics in public. In reality, these are the things that plague us daily. We are essentially encouraged to keep our conversations at a surface level. Human beings have unimaginable depth --so much so that few of us will ever actually fathom the true magnitude of our own existence. The truth is that going full-fledged adult is rife with responsibilities we aren't ready for, life altering situations that we can't make sense of, interacting with people who let us down, and dreams that never quite transcend into the physical world. We have got to start talking about these things if we ever want to step off the merry-go-round. Remember that it is the soul that acts as the light in your life. When the ego does it's best to keep aspects of yourself in the shadows, you must counteract that desire by pulling everything into the light. Every single one of these things is continuing to shape the ongoing narrative inside of our heads which will ultimately be expressed through our actions. What do your everyday actions say about what you really believe?

To the degree that we don't know ourselves is to the degree that we: 1. Aren't in control of our actions, and 2. Will continue to dwell on the inconsequential aspects of life that don't matter. You have to know yourself if you want to have any hope of knowing what really matters. Since our value system is individually held, it is only you that can decide what really matters to you.

Furthermore, we have to talk about all of the things with which we struggle so that we can form a worldview that will allow us to make sense of it all. Our incomplete view of the world around us caused by our repression and denying causes us to place an emphasis on the wrong things. To understand this properly, look no further than the death sentence that we associate with failure. We build it up so much in our minds that we are petrified of even considering the possibility of failure. The reality is that failure is just as much a part of the human experience as breathing or laughing. Yet our incorrect framing has built a risk averse society that trembles at the thought of its own dreams. Our skewed view of ourselves and our lives causes us to live as a shell of what we could be, as we maneuver around everything of which we are afraid. Our own fear is what boxes us in and minimizes our legacy.

The truth is that failure is much more of a fork in the road, then it is a roadblock. We would be much better off learning to make sense of our failures so that we can move forward and continue to forge on without retreating to a lesser life. A proper view of the world will help you do that. That is the power in finding the correct perspective.

Most of us spend our time defending our thoughts and world view instead of listening to the other side. The ego will dig its heels in in order to bolster its own view while the soul will be open to understanding. The ego will have us convinced that we are correct even if it's not serving us. What we must remember is that the information that can change your life is what you do not yet know. If what you knew were sufficient, you would be self- actualized and not reading this book. You don't have to suspend reason, only learn to hold space for the fact that the most important information in the world is what you don't know. This should be regardless of how bad the human side of you, the ego, wants to build itself up with self-importance and being correct.

In contrast, when things go right as opposed to failure, we become susceptible to losing ourselves in the success. The ego will conflate our success with our self-worth and then we end up giving our identity away to something that doesn't deserve it. This happens when we define ourselves by our current successes. When what goes up inevitably comes down, we revert back to the first scenario. You can see the roller coaster of emotion that the ego causes us to live on. It's a life that is defined by always chasing yet never feeling the satisfaction of attaining what's being chased. Quite frankly, it's exhausting.

Many of us live our lives with unimaginable potential, yet unimaginable is all it will ever be because we've never developed the ability to pick the path that would allow it to blossom and we're afraid of the adversity that will allow us to forge it. Hard work, technical prowess, good habits, even high intelligence, plus a litany of other traits that are professed to make you more successful in a multitude of life's arenas do you no good if you can't mentally reconcile the events that take place within the course of your life and find somewhere productive to put those experiences. The truth is, when you talk about success from a societal point of view, well-being and a sense of meaning never seem to make the list, yet we are all hoping for it. While the character traits that will breed success from a material perspective are quite well known, the ability to navigate those traits and still contend with our own humanity is a dance that requires much more grace.

The ego has been left to keep the soul captive while you are asleep. It will make a mess of things out of fear and not knowing what should be truly valued. Like all things that are truly free, however, this captivity won't last. If you seek it, you will eventually wake up to what your deepest desires for your life are. At that point your path will begin to change.

The soul understands that you need all of the lessons and drama that the ego is creating because of what you'll learn as a result of what you go through. For this reason, the soul is content to sit back while the ego makes a mess of things, telling itself that it's in charge. It will keep driving you to attain more things that it can rest its identity on, while the soul understands that it is only experience and a deep inner knowing that will help us form a true picture of ourselves. The painful part is that the experience you might need to clarify what matters is bouncing off of rock bottom as a result of living out of the ego.

True identity is always found when you release the desires of the ego and free yourself up to find a higher perspective. Understand that it is only you that can decide to begin walking down that path. This doesn't mean that you won't find happiness when you are living inside of the ego, because you will. You will find tons of pleasure as well. What you won't find is lasting joy. Joy comes to us a result of finding meaning. Meaning will come when you live in a way that aligns your value system with your character.

It's been said that all of the fear in the world can be traced back to the fear of death. It wouldn't matter nearly as much when things went wrong if you knew deep down that everything was ultimately going to be ok but the cliff that we're all heading toward creates a rather large amount of anxiety. Your ego is deeply human. It is the part of you that exists here in the physical space. Deep down it understands that it won't be making the trek with you to the other side when the hourglass finally runs out of sand. All the grasping and attaining are an attempt to root your ego in something solid -- something that exists here. It is like an hourglass in the way that it can try it's hardest to keep a choke hold on the middle, but the sand just keeps falling. Each grain of sand brings with it a little more anxiety about how much might be left. The soul understands what its current keeper does not. What you bring with you after you're gone isn't what the ego can attain, but instead, what the soul can become. The cliff you're heading toward is more of a liberation to the soul than it is an ending and so the urgency held by the ego isn't shared by the soul.

Chapter 5

BORN FOR WONDER

"Suddenly you're ripped into being alive. And life is pain, and life is suffering, and life is horror but my God you're alive and it's spectacular."

— Joseph Campbell

From the time that we're born we look at the world with wide-eyed wonder. It all starts when we're thrust into a new reality for which we don't feel ready. In fact, this is the first time of many in your life that you were completely equipped for something that you didn't feel ready. You had all the basics; the ability to process oxygen, consume nutrients, and to adapt to a new environment, if only for a little nurturing. What you lacked was the tactical knowledge about how to be in the world. Communication and movement patterns were clumsy, and you had to learn to process that information of which you were exposed. Yet, despite the lack of understanding about the world, you persisted and here you are -- reading a book about how you are.

You've unquestionably come a long way since infancy, and while that's not groundbreaking, what's important to understand is that you were born for this life. A concept so literal that every one of us loses track of its metaphorical implications. Realistically, what that means is that since day zero you've been scavenging the unknown for information and then assimilating to the unknown based on what you've learned. You've been doing this since long before you knew what it actually meant to learn something. It is when we allow our imagination to trample along the edge of what we know that we're able to map out the wild. Humans find their niche as we engage with what we've mapped out. This is the process of adaptation and you, just like everyone you know, have been specifically positioned for it. We are literally born to take on a world we don't feel ready for. You should be careful not to forget this when you are scared to pivot or take on a new role in life. Being ready for something in life isn't about being perfect, it's about being willing and teachable. It's about having the right amount of nurture to fully express your nature.

When we are in this infantile state, we contain the full spectrum of human emotions. To know this, all you have to do is spend a little time hanging around a baby. If they are stimulated enough, in a matter of about ten minutes, they will run through every emotion known to man. Since babies haven't learned to regulate their emotions (similar to many adults), and because they have an inability to communicate what it is they need (also similar to many adults), they end up wearing every one of those emotions on their facial expressions. Regardless of how you feel and think in your inner world, if you aren't able to communicate those feelings to the world around you, then your outer self (the one facing your friends, family, and co-workers) will always feel misunderstood. Communication is how we give birth to the thoughts that we've deemed worthy of reality. Improving communication is a prerequisite for an exquisite human experience. How you communicate is how you are perceived.

We're always staring out at the world of infinity and trying to make sense of it with our finite minds. This is the fundamental role of wonder in our lives. Lots of people take this ability for granted, and believe that all humans come to it innately. What we rarely stop to notice is just how much utility our own wonder has for us. In short, wonder is the way that we theorize how we are going to contend with what we don't yet know. It is the part of our mind that can imagine different outcomes, and then begin ordering them in order to make sense of them. At its best, wonder is soaked in possibility for upward mobility (whatever upward happens to mean to you). At our best, we lean into wonder and use it as a tool for navigating the world. Wonder allows you to look at the parts of your life that are incredibly unrefined and see what's beautiful about them. It's the first step in drawing a bridge from where you are to where you want to be and it is a free resource that we can all access. Just like other parts of our humanity, however, we won't have control of it if we spend our entire lives denying and repressing it.

Children are told repeatedly while growing up to stop daydreaming. Essentially, to stop using their imagination. What you will find is that this rhetoric is often espoused by people who had their own creative intelligence stifled. If you want to understand human nature, start by understanding that we are chameleons that propagate the lessons that we are exposed to, often against our best judgement. If someone has their evolution or growth stifled in any area throughout their lives, they are far more likely to do the same to others. The same goes for anything you might be exposed to while developing. If you grow up religious, you are far more likely to raise your kids that way and the same goes for being molested as a child. That is why generational trauma is difficult to break. It's easy to believe that our nature is always affected by a subjective understanding of right and wrong when in fact, it's more accurate to describe it as being predominantly affected by what has been and what hasn't been.

The fully integrated person is the one who can take what they are receiving and actually choose how to interpret and respond to it. They no longer act on individual emotions and wounds but instead can conceptualize why they are feeling what they are feeling. From that, they can then choose to act in a way that is by their own volition and not out of what they think they need to do in order to survive. That is how hurt people stop hurting people. They inventory their feelings and emotions and dispositions to know which characteristics are serving them and which need some reparenting. The less integrated your personality, the more of a need you have to expose yourself to positive narratives that you want to adopt. While no one can stand to be in a toxic environment 24/7, someone that has done the work to integrate the different aspects of their personality and who has become secure in his identity has much less of a chance of having his mood and feelings toward himself subjected to the whims of the world around him.

While you are looking to make changes or grow or pivot toward something else in life, it is imperative that you only consume information that is actually helpful and positive. Whatever your life looks like now is a reflection of the soil that you have maintained. If you try to grow something new in that same soil, you can't be too surprised when you have a hard time doing so and achieving success. We become what we're exposed to, and so in some sense, if you don't like who you've become, then you have to expose yourself to alternate settings. What this means for you is that if you are having trouble seeing options for your life, then it is because your environment isn't maintained in a way that allows you to see the options. If you truly decide that it is time to grow and you are committed to getting through all of the discomfort that true growth requires, then it may be time to find a new place to be planted as well. You won't be able to dance with your imagination and sift through what is and is not helpful if you spend your time trying to defend your new thoughts before you can even act on them.

This is all true for adults. For children, we have the opportunity to teach them these things from the beginning. Re-learning how to use your imagination as an adult can change your life immensely, but teaching people to use it from the beginning could put them on an entirely new path. This path has the possibility of what could be, and isn't hindered by what never was, from the generation before them. This is why one of the most crippling things you can do to a human is to take away their ability to imagine. Many people have many reasons for stripping the ability of wonder from the youth around them, but what you find is that it almost always goes back to them having had the same thing happen to them. We don't often think of this as generational trauma, but make no mistake about the fact that it is. If you step back and consider what you're asking when you tell someone to stop daydreaming, you'll see how traumatic it really is. Kids have a natural inclination to wonder so that they can make sense of the world and draw a bridge from their thoughts to their reality. We are creating a lot of disconnected and unintegrated humans by stripping them of that ability. Instead, we program ridges around their thoughts and they end up feeling badly for what they naturally want to do. We collectively do this to so many children in the name of formal schooling, corporate religion, and good order and discipline on such a grand scale, we are dimming the world's light by orders of magnitude.

Should we decide to bolster the wonder of our youth (as well as our own), there is no telling what products, services, or acts of unbelievable proportion we're missing. To expand the collective consciousness of the world, everyone that is in it must feel like they are free to let their thinking roam free. We will never grow if we are punished every time we expand. How many Elon Musks out there are working in accounting on the ninth floor of a corporation that produces widgets for the masses because they were told how ridiculous it would be to try and inhabit Mars? Lots of people have incredible ideas about what life could look like, but they are trapped inside of a thought pattern that won't allow them to explore it. Now they are funneling their creativity into squeezing more money out of government regulations, instead of pushing our species into new frontiers.

Another reason that people stifle a child's ability to imagine things is the same reason that someone would ever clip any bird's wings – you are afraid it will fly away and the part of you that's insecure and afraid to lose it or lose the ability to control it, makes the decision to leverage power by force to get what it wants. Every weak minded leader in history has used the same tactic. At the highest expression of who we are, humans can conceive of a way to get ourselves on the moon. At our lowest, we get Auschwitz. Are you using your creative intelligence to build cages or launch pads? In a world where Hell is always around the corner, it seems incredibly destructive to take away someone's ability to cope and generate their own hope. Every time you tell someone to stop daydreaming, you are chipping away at one of the greatest human gifts.

Your ability to wonder is directly correlated with your ability to create your life in the way that you wanted. It is the best tool that you have for coming to grips with transcending the outer edge of your reality. Like a tool, it can be made sharper or duller. It all depends on the way that you apply pressure to the blade.

It is worth taking a moment to think about how you have personally applied pressure to your own blade. Do you allow your mind to wander in wonder and become solution-oriented, or do you simply beat yourself up for being in such a negative situation? How are you applying pressure to your own blade? The wrong pressure will leave you ineffective. Something worth knowing about yourself is that you can't possibly perform at your best while simultaneously beating yourself up for not performing at your best. You can't be happier by pointing out all of the reasons that you can't be happy. You also can't use your mind for good and give it the freedom to find the right solution or perspective if you are constantly ridiculing it for where it travels. Each of these scenarios, although quite common, is an example of applying the wrong type of pressure to your blade. Free thought is always the substance behind the fabric of revolution. If you want to revolutionize your own life, you may need to set your thoughts free.

Ridicule is self-directed when people have a poor understanding of the role of their own minds in their lives. The mind is the rationalizing part of you that adds judgment to what the eyes see. That judgement is further decided to be good or bad by you -- the being behind the mind. The mind simply gives you a narrative about everything that happens in your life so that you can understand where you are. It adds context to life so you can orient yourself in the world.

Some of that context will be cemented in your psyche when it is sure of what it has experienced. It tells you that a bed is for sleeping and a phone is for talking (or used to be). It is your mind that knows this as soon as you see those things, based on the context you've experienced in the past. Choosing to believe a certain narrative is the choice that you get in this life.

Remember that from the time we are born, we are always scavenging our environment for information that will help us navigate it. It is important that we remember this and use what we find for what it actually is; objective information about the world around us. The narrative that your mind attaches to the things around you says nothing about who you are as a person or your worth. When the mind is used as it's supposed to be, it gives you objective context for the present moment based on past experience. You know you are giving your mind too much agency over your life when the information grows subjective. We tend to act as if the past says something about us, independent of the world. What is actually true is that the past only holds information about how you engaged with the world in the past. Your entire life is a series of subject/object relationships with everyone and everything around you. If you don't like something that has transpired in the past, it is unproductive (not to mention inaccurate) to try and label yourself based on it. If you are a loser, what hope do you have to start winning in the future? If you recognize that you acted a certain way in the past, and that way has resulted in loss, then you are positioned to reparent yourself around those scenarios in the future. This will improve your relationship with your life. Inner growth is about continuously being able to do that.

The past is something that no longer exists except for in your mind. It is only you who insists on dragging it into the present moment, and it is only you that can allow it to say something about your character today. The past contains information about how to proceed with the moment. However, after some reflection, if we don't leave the past alone, it will hijack our moments and eventually our future. As you orient yourself and make your way in the world, the mind continues to do what it does, adding a narrative to things so that you can understand them. Over time you slowly learn what's acceptable and what's not. The problem is that outside of survival, the mind doesn't really have an agenda. The mind is often just throwing stuff at the wall to see what sticks. If the narrative makes sense to you, and matches the reality that you've come to know, then it will likely be cemented as you adopt it. It is important that you understand that your current existence is a result of the current narratives that you are living out. Every time your mind spins up a narrative, it is you who chooses to adopt that narrative. Once you do, it is you who will live it out. Often our minds will tell us something counterproductive, and we will believe it without ever asking ourselves if the thought is productive or if we even want it in our heads. Again, usually when our mind starts spinning, we actually feel like we are at the behest of that narrative. It will confirm its own bias or what it comes up with and it will keep spinning further and further from a place of peace or contentment.

One of the mind's chief characteristics is that it loves to fall in love with its own ideas. It will find more and more things to worry about and because we live in a world with endless possibilities, it will continue to point out what's wrong and what isn't helping. When this happens, we often feel powerless against stopping it. What might help is if you start to understand that this is the exact moment when a human has a chance to take the driver's seat in his own life. You have the ability to tell your mind what to do, but what you don't have is the ability to tell it what not to do. If you don't believe me, try it right now. Tell yourself not to think about something, anything, and just see how that works out for you.

This concept is instrumental in knowing how to change directions in life. It is here that you have the chance to reparent yourself, and change your relationship with the narratives in your life. If the narratives that your mind is spinning up aren't actually helping, all of the self-denying in the world will be useless. For example, if you have an underlying belief that you are a failure, the more that you try to tell yourself that you aren't a failure, the more you will focus on the fact that your mind has a belief that you are. You can redirect your attention to what you want to create but you can't tell yourself to stop focusing on the narratives that you've already created. Said simply, shift your focus to what works and what you want as opposed to what isn't working and what you don't want. Stop dwelling on what isn't serving your life and begin to look for what is. Psychologically, your brain is set up for that solution. When you identify areas in your life that aren't working for you, you have to take these moments to calmly search for alternative narratives, and then choose the one that you want to adopt. It's not always easy but it certainly is this simple.

You can choose to believe something different then you have believed your entire life. Limiting beliefs are blinding and lead you to believe that you are up against a legitimate wall as they create walls in your mind. If you want to change your reality, it is only your thinking that you must change. The rest will follow suit. Your mind will tell you something about failure, but you can choose the way in which you respond. Most people don't feel they have the ability to choose how they respond to something. Once again, that is just a misconception about how life works. What holds us back in reality are patterns, not reality itself.

As another example, if the narrative in your head is one that says failure isn't an option, whenever you run into an inevitable failure (whether that's a break up or an unfinished or unrealized project), your psyche is going to run into a wall. You will find it extremely difficult to ever move past this wall because you have convinced yourself you live in a world where failure isn't an option. You will keep searching for ways to make it right, or to justify what happened. You will find nothing, however, because failures are a part of life. You will be stuck wherever you are in your growth because your world view won't allow forward progress. You will just keep going back to the moment that you failed and searching for an angle that lets you keep your worldview intact -- the one that doesn't see you as a failure.

When people never move on from a breakup, it's often because they never emerge with a new world view that allows them to. It has very little, if anything, to do with the person that they're pining over. In this case, you may see that people want to get back to someone with whom they've broken up, even if they weren't particularly happy with the relationship, because their minds are convinced that they can "make it right" successfully getting them past the failure.

Truly moving forward happens as a result of inner healing. Healing begins when you can honestly look at the broken parts of your life and decide which can be fixed by fixing and which can be fixed by letting go. Start by letting go of your judgement about failure, and you'll start to see that you are free to move on. Once you change your relationship with what's gone wrong, you will get to the point where you understand that nothing has actually gone wrong. You have just positioned yourself in a way to learn through pain instead of love. Your ability to think through these tough situations in life is tied back to your ability to wonder and imagine. We must learn to ask ourselves, "This is what I am seeing, but what am I missing? What else might this mean?" It is not what you are going through that makes a difference in your life. It is how you are seeing yourself in relation to what you are going through. If you can imagine a different way to handle the situation, you can handle the situation differently. If you can't, you can't, and with that, you can understand the importance of the human's ability to wonder. The path you can't see has the answer you can't find.

When we are really young, say before twelve years of age or so, most of us haven't been indoctrinated into the world of negative media cycles and people who don't believe in our dreams. As a result, we tend to put our wonder in some really positive places. We wonder what we might be able to be when we grow up, and then we craft the answer with a reckless optimism that lights up our eyes with hope for the future. The key to a good life is allowing your wonder to be soaked in reverence for life itself. If you are going to choose to keep living in this life, then you have to decide that living is in itself, worth it. Any theory of the universe that leaves us questioning its point will always require a part of us to remain in contemplation. That is a part of ourselves that could be gaining momentum forward. Life is like anything else. If it is worth doing, it is worth doing well. Doing well is about how you do what you do. It is a mindset, not an achievement.

That is why we want to be heroes, or rock stars, or princesses when we are young. No one has told us yet that we can't, so our minds are still free to believe that we can. In reality, heroes and rock stars and princesses exist now, you are just not one of them because you won't allow yourself to be. Most people also don't know any of them because the soil they've planted themselves in also wouldn't allow people to be. You exist in a barren desert, and you've convinced yourself that flowers aren't real because you can't see any.

A crucial mistake in the human experience is taking all of the confusion and perplexing situations that we face and allowing the suspicion about what they mean to be hijacked by pessimistic narratives coming from people with a poor understanding of reality. Even painful situations in life can be acknowledged as painful without a pessimistic worldview. Failure can be the best or worst thing to ever happen to you. The kicker is that the only one who gets to decide is the person who is affected by it – you. You can marvel at the universe beyond your understanding with reverence and see all that it might hold for your life, or you can continue to fight it as if you are in an adversarial relationship with everything you don't understand. Again, the only person that can decide that is the person that's standing face to face with the unknown. That's still you.

People go around saying all kinds of things about the world in order to feel safe. Other drivers on the road are idiots, other countries are a threat to our way of life, other religions are derived from the devil. The more someone makes a negative absolute judgement about parts of the world around them, the more you can rest assured that they don't understand it. No one has ever done anything great by pointing out what the world lacks. No one has improved their life with that tactic either.

What's different than you is not stupid, or threatening, or evil. If you can get to the point where you believe that, you stand a chance at actually learning something. Never underestimate the fact that what the unknown will teach you is the thing that you need to know in order to change your life. That's one of the incredible truths that's built into the equation that runs the universe. The whole thing is set to give you what you need to grow if you have the courage to confront what you don't know.

If you want to know if someone is living a scared or frightened existence, keeping their consciousness smaller than it could be, you must only look to their relationship with the unknown. Our psychology has a built-in mechanism for finding negative situations. This is because the possibility always exists that the monster waiting in the unknown is ready to swallow you whole. Be that as it may, what history repeatedly teaches us is that there is no valor found in the chances that you don't take. Everything you could ever want is currently waiting beyond the horizon. You are just too scared to move past the horizon. Your life will be either boring or incredible, based on whether or not you decide to take up arms against the unknown. People that are afraid to confront the unknown will learn to make themselves feel better by bringing the world down around them. They are the kids that are too cool for school and always see themselves as above what they are doing. This is how they cope with their fear of engaging earnestly with a force that could take them out. Those same people will grow up to tell you what you can't do. When you are too good to be somewhere, you are never actually able to point out what's good about where you are. A life of being too cool for what's around you will leave you completely incapable of enjoying it. Valor is earned as you shoulder risk with your eyes forward and your chin up.

As we age we have a tendency to let the world negatively influence us much more. We vibrate at a lower frequency as we contend with cyclical thought patterns and as a result we begin to put our wonder in some really unfortunate places. We wonder if we will ever be good enough or if that person really likes us. We wonder if we will ever catch a break, or when will it finally be "our turn." The world has a way of turning our wonder from a place of excitement about ourselves to insecurities about how we will be perceived by everyone else. Suddenly our wonder, which used to be a source of hope, becomes the source of our anxiety. Untangling the feelings that rob you of your wellbeing starts by understanding that the root of all anxiety is the unknown. When we start looking at the unknown as if it is something to be feared, we give our anxiety the room it needs to grow. Our brains are staggeringly good at vivid visualization. We are good at fabricating the terror that could be lurking in the unknown, and it has a tendency to want to review that terror every time we have a quiet moment. Dealing with the unknown in life is just like everything else; it's made better or worse by where you choose to put your focus. If you focus on what could go wrong, the sense of wonder that you've been avoiding is likely to find itself heading in the wrong direction. In this case, the fear of what could go wrong is going to ruin your wellbeing far more than anything actually going wrong. You will make decisions based on fear. Those decisions will force you to avoid things you want, so that you can keep "the scaries" at bay. Most likely, your life will continue down this path because everything in our psyche works on momentum. Fear only begets more fear.

All of our lives we're told not to wonder, we're told to play it safe and to be reasonable in our expectations. To take this tact, however, is to forget from where we come. To be human is to risk. It is only through risk that you will gain what you don't yet have. The good news is that you had the skills to live this way since day one. You just have to commit to never having the "maybe I should have" conversation with yourself. You will know the people that don't make that commitment, because they will be the first ones to have the "maybe you shouldn't" conversation with you. When it comes to crafting a truly authentic life, that childlike wonder that we are taught to dismiss is the key to the entire thing. As we age and focus much more on responsibility and what we "have to do," we focus much less on every little feeling and thought that arises. We have semi-formed ideas about something we might want to do, or try at some point, or places we'd like to go, but we are taught to dismiss those thoughts as unimportant. We prioritize what people tell us to prioritize (specifically or implied), but more often than not, this results in us focusing on a whole lot of areas in our lives that aren't actually improving them.

Our hopes and dreams are deprioritized as we try to navigate the world without being ridiculed or looking stupid. Know that as long as you cling to what you've deduced as "reasonable," you will never be in a position to create a life that is incredible. What is incredible almost always falls outside of what society deems reasonable. You are not under any obligation to maintain a reasonable life by societies arbitrarily undefined metrics.

The path to the true self starts when you stop prioritizing the world's opinion over your own. The problem is that you have been contending with the world's opinion since day one. If you learn to listen to that small voice inside, what you'll find is that it isn't so small. It is your ticket to an authentic expression of you on this earth. In light of this fact, the question becomes, "How do you start actually listening to you and how do you deprioritize the person that the world wants you to be?" The person that you wonder if you could become and the things that you wonder if you could do, might just be the best place to start.

Chapter 6

OF THE WILD

"Much of human behavior can be explained by watching
the wild beasts around us. They are constantly
teaching us things about ourselves and the way of
the universe, but most people are too blind to
watch and listen."

— Suzy Kassem

The well developed society around us can make it easy to forget that the way that we live now is relatively new to our species. When a new generation is born, they take for granted the ease of life that they inherit and rarely stop to think about the sacrifices that were made from the generations before them. In the case of the human being, however, those hardships have been baked into his DNA over the course of million of years. What this means for us is that we evolved to be optimized for a world that we don't necessarily live in.

Perhaps, thousands of years from now, humanity will merge with technology and in that moment, we will be far less beholden to the nature from which we were born. As of this writing, that simply isn't the case. Regardless of the advancements in biotechnology, we will remain at the demands of a breathing, sweating, monkey suit, and if we want our lives to function optimally, then we must give it what it needs. The current state of the human condition can never be fully separate from the nature from which we evolved. Our predilections, behaviors, and even spirit must remain somewhat in concert with the ebb and flow of the earth that we came out of. When we become too synthetic, and spend too much time manipulating our biology, it is usually our wellbeing that pays the price.

In my observation, the human animal functions at its peak when it returns to its more primitive inhabitants, even if only for a moment. Amidst the mountains and jungles, the mind has room to roam just as the body does. The detox from our synthetic lives provides clarity to think and establish order where chaos has a habit of building during our commuting and our bill paying and our TPS reports. The stress hormone, cortisol, was originally meant to help you evade the parts of nature that want to kill you, not nature all together. It is produced in the body during times of stress in order to stimulate a response and get you to a less stressful environment where things aren't quite as dangerous. When its production is rampant, that is usually a hint that we are no longer in concert with our nature. The lights and screens that rule our life tend to throw the animal in us out of whack so we use uppers to function, downers to sleep it off, and therapy to help us cope with the world that we've built.

Looking out across the oceans or up into the stars makes us feel small yet centered because deep down there is a recognition of self. We are made primarily of the same things that fell from the sky and that fills the ocean. Our matter is simply organized differently, for the time being. To consider that we come from and will eventually be reabsorbed in nature, is it unreasonable to believe that our current lives can't be improved by that same force? If you want to get a little closer to knowing the real you that's been buried beneath the weight of the world and the social pressure of your environment, you don't have to look further than the wild that is butted up against our cities. Simply observing it quells the spirit and increases the chemicals in your brain that are associated with an increase in positive mood. The facade and the fake have a way of making us feel out of sorts because although that is what we construct, it's not necessarily what we are constructed for.

It doesn't always take some vast undertaking to begin rediscovering yourself or even to begin discovering yourself for the first time. Simply park your car at the edge of the wood line, and begin to make your way into the unknown while traveling on foot. In only a short time, you will find that what is unknown was always known. It was just buried at a level that's too deep to access.

As we grapple with our own nature, humans find that we have to exist in an unsettling paradox. On one hand, our very being was forged in the animal kingdom. Before the formation of the frontal lobe and the eventual industrialization of our playground, we prevailed in the ultimate game of savagery; survival of the fittest. Long before Under Armor or Nike, it was our bare feet that endured the abuse of the primitive ground. Looking at the mountains now, they serve as a fossilized backbone of a prehistoric time. A time that saw humans proving their worth with their legs, lungs and grit. Now we have a mind that is capable of looking and assessing itself and adding judgement to the subject / object relationship of our being. As consciousness has evolved, so has the knowledge of the limitations of our own existence. We are aware of our own existential crisis. Beyond that, we are developed enough to look at our own nature and try to curb it to appease the masses. Despite the efforts of even the most civilized among us, our nature won't ever be fully curbed as we are very much still dealing with biological baggage that developed during our earlier fight for survival.

The world which developed us consisted of a landscape where the demands, although rigorous, were actually far simpler than they are now. All we needed to survive was to know whether we should stay and fight in the presence of danger or whether we should run. After all, our sympathetic nervous system was not developed so that we could fight our bosses or flee the office. That just happens to be what we use it for now. Much of our problems arise from the fact that the intellectual complexities of our current world tend to overwhelm us and make it difficult to find clarity. Our bandwidth is limited to contend in proportion to the demands that we are now placing on it. You can't read and talk about something else at the same time. You also can't contend with the many inputs that are vying for your emotional bandwidth and still successfully process the emotions you are feeling now at the same time.

Lots of people are fighting multiple battles internally every day and it causes chaos between their ears. People are simultaneously upset about not being chosen by their last partner, trying to be who their new partner wants them to be, doing the same thing for their parents, and trying to perform at work. This occurs all while trying to converse and hold space for their friend who is going through the same thing. Most people are self-centered because their self is actually so far off center that they can't possibly process anything else. Sometimes a walk back into nature satiates the soul because things become simpler as the world we've manufactured fades into the background. We must never underestimate the recognition of home and the power that it has to quell our troubles. Just seeing the color green has been associated with a positive increase in overall mood for many humans. You simply weren't evolved for the stressors you have adopted.

All of our introspective analyzing and assimilating has left us much more civilized. At least that is what we tell ourselves. With our newfound ability to comprehend the ramifications of our actions, we've developed coping mechanisms that see our nature for its primal actuality and constantly attempt to shove it deep down. We often minimize our own qualities and hope no one will ever know us for who we truly are.

Our surroundings no longer require the savagery that they once did, so we are left to explain away and subdue the sides of us that are still more beast than human. Pretending you don't have an animalistic nature doesn't make it so, it only makes it so you don't get to control its expression. In the way life always seems to balance itself out -- what goes up always comes down -- what we bury will eventually resurface. Just like a seed can resurface as a great oak tree, so to do our repressed feelings and urges resurface as something bigger, something greater in the worst sense of the word. Our attempts to muddle and suppress what we really want and who we really are can manifest down the road as much of what ails the human condition. This includes physical illness, character traits that we can't understand ourselves, depression and at times dependence or abuse. By never getting to know the wild side of ourselves, we end up acting like (and eventually becoming) someone that we don't know at all.

To put something as vast as the human experience into words is no easy undertaking. From time to time, it will be eloquent and descriptive. From time to time, it will be brutish and encumbered. Fitting, as this is exactly the way that life works out for so many of us as we try to navigate between the chaos and structure of our lives. We're psychologically and biologically standing with one foot in the wilderness and one foot in society at all times. Taking into consideration the animal that lives within us all, one could make a great case for rejecting the society that we've constructed. Yet, it is our desire to continue to evolve our own species that keeps us paving over the wild from where we came. Further, it is our own deep seated desire for survival, forged in those early years, that ensures we fall into routines on the pavement that we lay. The optimal conditions for being are somewhere in the middle of the chaos we come from and the structure we create to deal with it. Our lives are in a never ending relationship with the people and the things that are around us. The quality of our lives are forged based on how we choose to manage those relationships. The human paradox requires that we are always walking a fine line between opposing worlds, but our adaptable nature means that we are extremely susceptible to being consumed by those worlds as well.

When we are around uplifting people, and high vibrational or philosophical conversations, we feel it in our resonance. Our consciousness expands and our vitality is rejuvenated. That same consciousness is diminished by low vibrational conversations such as gossip. This is the case for delayed gratification. It may make you feel better to join in on low vibrational conversations because of the temporary boost in ego identity, but ultimately, a life of gossip isn't actually in line with what most people want for their lives. What and who we choose to interact with while we're here permeates every facet of our being. When you stay in toxic environments, it begins to affect your psychology rather quickly. That mental toll will of course find its way into your physiology as well. The way we feel about how we show up in time and space is influenced most by the decisions that we make and our relationship with our environment.

In modern society, the environment we are creating is putting us into a tricky situation. We are both the animal and the zookeeper. Just like with any zoo, we often have to drug ourselves to cope with the walls around us that we've constructed. The only difference between the actual zoo and most of us that work unhappy office jobs, is that our cage isn't actually locked. Even our eyesight, which was developed to look over horizons and up into trees, degenerates as we constantly stare at the four walls around us. We shouldn't be so surprised when we lose the ability to contend with what comes over the horizon when we spend our lives avoiding it. Instead of disavowing the aspects of us that resonate with the wild, there is much to be gained from studying it. We have a clear innate desire to continue pushing and evolving our species. In the same way we went from savage to sophistication, you can continue to evolve your own life.

What you find in common human qualities, is a deep desire to continuously map out and pave the wild. We are living this out from the time we are kids, which is why one of the proper roles of a parent is to encourage children to go out and engage with the world. Kids may get hurt in this process, but not nearly as much as if they were to lose the ability to contend with risk on their own terms. We must always seek to find our own limitations if we ever want to figure out how to surpass them. You have to test out the environment around you so that you know what is safe and what isn't, and where you stand amidst it all.

If you never step into the unknown, you run the risk of growing too fearful of it. If the unknown starts to represent something that you can't go near, you will find limitations to who you are and what you can do that are far below your innate limits. This is because everything we will encounter in life has some sort of an unknown element. We just happen to be equipped with a psyche that is capable of contending with it... if only with a little practice. How many adults are downright terrified of the unknown? How many adults are stuck in a toxic environment simply because they perceive it as safe and have never gathered the skills to find out otherwise? We see it with friends, romantic relationships, and professions that aren't serving the soul. Most people would rather sit in known misery than confront what they don't know, on the off chance that what they don't know holds possible catastrophe. The denial and inability to engage with the world in the way we were meant is causing us to feel stuck where we are.

Anyone who has spent time in the wild comes to understand that what is taking place in the psyche transcends the physical world that we are able to see and touch. The human spirit has an infinite energy buried deep within it that is capable of overcoming staggering odds. It is an energy that will not be denied once tapped. It is a flow state, it is potential, it is an indomitable will, and it is an unconquerable soul. You have it innate within you just as much as the next human. You will find it only when you put yourself in a situation that demands its presence.

Chapter 7

ON BECOMING

Evidence consistently suggests that just because you don't remember something, doesn't mean that it doesn't guide your behavior. What you've learned to be true at one time might no longer currently work for you and your life, you may have dismissed it from your awareness, but you may still be carrying out actions as if it is still true. This is seen when we get our heart broken by a lover, and then have trouble in the future giving someone else that same level of intimacy. The new relationship ultimately falls apart. Your partner cites the fact that you aren't willing to let them in as the reason for the failure. You know she is right, but you don't know why. You just silently ask yourself, "What the hell is wrong with me?" And then you move on.

It is difficult to know how deep that actual belief really is and where it is stemming from. If you happened to witness your parents with relationship issues, and then your adult world experiences confirm those suspicions, that particular belief could be buried way down below many layers of consciousness. What this means is that you could be completely unaware of why you do what you do. You'll feel like an autonomous being that is making all of your own decisions when in reality, something in the past is architecting not only what you are doing but is also contributing to the underlying emotion that is guiding your reason for doing it in the first place. It could also be that your parents constantly put you in the middle of their relationship problems. In that case, there are probably certain triggers in relationships that make you feel like you are going to have to go back to having the pressure of a failing relationship on your shoulders, like you did when you were five years old.

When you are triggered from a certain experience, the ego will perform at whatever level and age you were when you learned how to survive that particular situation. When adults throw temper tantrums over things that seem incredulous to you, now you know why. The ego needs to be slowly taught that it exists in a new environment. That old behavior is no longer needed or helpful. Remember, the ego is made from patterns of conditioned thought. You have to teach it that those patterns are not relevant to the present moment if you want to act differently. If you don't, your ego and your subconscious will live in an echo chamber all of your life, consistently confirming their own biases about the world. "See, you can't have a good long term relationship. That's why we have to protect ourselves." The story gets deeper and deeper, each layer of thought more ingrained. The story can only be changed when we realize that it is only us who confirms the bias.

You are both the problem and the solution. What is between those two realizations is the awareness of your own behavior and the death of who your ego has led you to believe you are. You must let go of the story you are telling yourself about the world if you want it to act differently within it. What we truly believe is made up of a combination of what we have been conditioned to believe, and what we have encountered to be true, after bouncing those beliefs off of our own experience. That belief is then shifted into the subconscious to make room for new information. It then becomes a pattern that you act out. It can be helpful to think of your subconscious as being influenced by a set of patterns that build a flow chart. Your brain is referencing this flow chart at lightning fast speeds as you motor along though the world.

To get a clear idea about how these patterns work, let's use the oft referenced hot stove example. While you were growing up (when your subconscious is thought to be the most impressionable), your mother and father told you repeatedly not to touch the stove while the burner was hot. At some point, however, curiosity got the best of you. Eventually, when no one was looking, you finally did reach up and touch the red rings. Unsurprisingly, just like you were told, you burned yourself. Then your parents came over and put a cold compress on the burn or ran it under cold water while calmly explaining to you that this is why we don't touch hot things.

A flow chart of sorts was just ingrained deep within you. If hot, don't touch. If burned, run under cold water. You were raised to believe it, that belief measured up to your real world experience, and *voila*, it is cemented as intrinsic truth in your reality.

These sorts of patterns have been programmed into you at every point of your life. They have to do with every aspect of your character, thought patterns, and mode of being in the world. "If hot, don't touch" is also, "if in need, pray," or, "if upset, confront the person making you upset (or not)," or, "if hurt by someone, hurt someone else." How you were programmed and how you perceived that programming when it was subjected to real world experience is all cemented into your very being.

Of course, for many things, this programming is necessary. The hope is that your parents were able to program useful things in your life, so that you can make your way in the world and live a good life. You don't want to go around touching every hot thing that glows for the next ten years, programming yourself the hard way. For much of the information we perceive, the subconscious (also known as the adaptive unconscious) and its selecting mechanisms are important. In addition to not touching the hot stove, you also don't want to sit there and recall why you shouldn't, or have to go into meditation over it every time that situation confronts you.

The issue in this arises when you are conditioned to believe things about the way that the world works, based on someone else's understanding. For example, if your parent's belief is that life is a zero sum game, (in order for someone to win, someone else must lose), then most likely, those are the rules that you are playing by as well. The inferred narrative of that belief is that in order for you to gain, you have to take from someone else. If you happen to intrinsically value material success so much so that your ego depends on it, then you might find yourself acting this out at all costs.

You can find yourself going against your better judgment and taking from people that you care about in order to further the agenda of your subconscious. It is worth pointing out that this example doesn't necessarily mean taking something physical. Our ego's need for validation is often shown when we belittle, take someone else's energy or slight a partner. This is often how we hurt people we love or do things that we ourselves despise. It is happening outside of our awareness and because we haven't taken the time to recognize all that drives our behavior in an attempt to bring it into alignment with our actual intentions, the behavior will continue.

When we have real friction in life it is often due to the fact that our intrinsic value system is out of alignment with our ego. Perhaps we value relationships and the ego is constantly ruining those in order to self soothe or survive. If your past was tumultuous, then you have to understand that the ego is comfortable in dealing with that chaos. Your conditioned thoughts and beliefs are built in that environment. When people exhibit self-destructive behavior, it is often because they don't know how to think in order to thrive. They constantly put themselves back in a survival situation because it is what they know. Your life is a result of what you've been conditioned to accept or endure. If you want something else, then you have to condition yourself to receive something else. If deep down, the thought process that you act out doesn't resonate with what you really want, you will live with constant turmoil. You will want one thing, but have such deeply ingrained patterns to the contrary that actually getting it is going to be next to impossible. You can see with a very basic example, how complex and deep this problem can get.

We often observe this with money and people's associated beliefs. If our parents have an adverse relationship with money, that relationship is also passed along to us. When we try to make money of our own and find it difficult (which is no surprise when we were taught to earn it from someone who resented that process), our thought conditioning is then cemented. We bounce what we learned off our own experiences and found the belief to be true. This pattern then molds part of our psyche into a certain way of being. Whether or not this way is actually serving us is irrelevant to the subconscious. It acts on what it knows and what it knows has kept you alive so far. Your subconscious isn't concerned with worldly metrics like your ego is. It doesn't give a damn whether or not you make money or are successful in the long run. For all its complexities, the subconscious just doesn't have the capacity to plan for the future. It knows survival in this moment, and that is where it is comfortable. The subconscious could never see the value in planting a seed, for example.

It is important that you live your life on your terms and not the terms of our oldest thought pattern. This is especially true if you ever want to reap the benefits of what you plant today. If your subconscious is comfortable, it knows that it is surviving and it will continue to put you in that place. Even if comfortable means living in constant turmoil, drama, or chaos. We see this played out with people that seem to be addicted to having these things in their own life. They legitimately are. From the outside, it's easy to see how negative someone's behavior actually is, but on the inside, it is a fight for survival.

Another way that our mind works is by reasoning that if we are able to judge something before it has a chance to unfold, we can maintain mental order by understanding what that thing is, and keep it where we've mentally filed it. We do the same thing with the people in our lives. Most people will not see you for who you are but instead will see you for the very first mental picture that they formed of you. If you are trying to grow into a new mode of being in the world and find that the people that are regularly around you aren't necessarily recognizing you for who you are but are treating you like who you were, this is why.

In essence we feel safe around things that we understand. The less we understand, the less safe we feel to make moves. People suffering from an existential dread have trouble picking a path for this reason. Their lack of judgement about what it all means leaves them feeling incredibly unsafe. Coincidentally, this is why it is so important that humans work through the things that they are feeling and thinking. We have to know when a thought or belief is no longer serving us. If we keep our mental picture together by disparaging others, then our picture of the world is disparaging ourselves. The way our world is set up, everything around you is a karmic net where whatever it is you throw into it, you get back yourself. If you are the guy or girl complaining about everything that is around you, then you are the girl or guy that is living in a world where everything is constantly wrong.

The primary function of the mind is to rationalize and judge everything so that we know where it stands and what it means. In the beginning of this book, we referenced this mental picture that we are always trying to hold on to as coherence. Without it, taking any action at all is nearly impossible because you won't know in which direction it is safe to move. Mentally, "1 + 1 + 1" always has to equal "3" in our minds. In our lives this looks like us understanding why one behavior plus another plus another lead us to a desired outcome. We have to know why things happen. When things are really wrong for you, it is often because you have lost coherence in your world, and now everything is left up for questioning. If a friend betrays you, and she does something you would never condone, you have to ask yourself, "Is she really who I thought she was?" If she isn't, then perhaps you aren't who you thought you were either? If that is the case, then maybe the world isn't what you thought it was either. This is what happens when the reasoning mind begins to lose it's reasons.

Cynicism happens when our world falls apart and we have to then regain coherence. If we can't find a good reason for why things fell apart, we're likely to simplify it and tell ourselves that it's because people are inherently bad. Or because the world is set up for people to fail. Or because the opposite sex is dumb. This cynicism is often a survival mechanism because we depend so heavily on coherence that if we don't regain, we'll find it too difficult to go on. We assume everyone has the ability to hurt us and maybe we believe they will if we are naive enough to let them. Our cynical world view now allows us to resume living life, even if it comes at the cost of our mental health. The truth is that everyone, including you, has the capacity to do anything. A productive worldview holds space for that so that cynicism isn't always necessary.

Laying the foundation for your life is actually supposed to be the easy part. Getting wherever it is in life that you want to get is the part that takes tact, the development of skill and the compounding of hard work. Most people don't get where they want, however, because they can't get the foundation of their beliefs laid in a way that they can build on. Instead of forward progress, they are holding on to their simplified view of people and the world. This causes them, in some cases, to have to recapitulate their picture every few years or even months.

The next belief to regain coherence is understanding that people are going to hurt others but that is about them, not you. They are in an adversarial relationship with life just like you are when you live out of the ego. You just might have happened to get caught in their shadows this time. Recognize this so you can move on and get back to your own internal work..

If you understand that everyone needs coherence, you can also better understand why some people are less than supportive of your growth. We have all mapped the world out in a certain way and now our well-being is contingent on that map remaining accurate. When people try to stifle your growth, it is often because they have bounced who they are off of who you are, and they are comfortable with that picture. If you are capable of more than that means they might be as well. If you want growth by starting a new project, or business, or adopting a new workout routine, then you are volunteering for change. The people around you might not be ready for that change and they will resist their mental picture of the world changing as a result. This isn't a reason to stifle your own growth, but rather to help you show grace to others that aren't supporting your growth like you had assumed that they would.

Often when we disparage others, it is an attempt by the ego to remain what we think we are. The ego is always planting flags in the ground, not only to let others know that the land is ours, but to feel safe on the ground in the first place. This is why we choose to identify ourselves by our jobs, titles, or our accomplishments. If you identify yourself by anything in this world, part of you is remaining there in that place with that thing. If you can understand this and let it go, you can free yourself up to exist in the present moment. If you bring all of you here now, to this moment, you won't need to go searching for where else you might be.

The question to ask yourself is, "Are you willing to remain with the same feeling of safety at the price of existing in a false reality?" The ego is centered around "I", meaning it really doesn't have the bandwidth or time to sit down and understand everyone's individual nuances (including your own). Instead, we gain a mental picture of someone (accurate or not) and then we continue to project that image on to them. When someone makes a massive change in life, it is difficult for others because maintaining a projection over top of an evolving entity is impossible. When either us or the people in our lives decide to take on change, it feels destabilizing because it hints at the bigger picture: The self is always in flux, life is always evolving, and everything within it is always changing. You can free yourself of mental torment by understanding that all of this has been learned and therefore, may be unlearned. This applies to our own patterns of being, as well as the way that we are interpreting the patterns of others.

Aside from regaining your own sanity, the inherent problem with judgement about others is that humans aren't smart enough to have it. The finite nature of our awareness means that whatever we judge something by can only be a representation of the current picture or lens we are looking through. What time always reveals is a more complete picture of what is.

Right now, you can picture anyone you might want to in your mind. Someone you hate, someone you love, or someone to whom you are indifferent. Regardless of how you feel about anyone, what you want to understand is that you don't fully understand them. It's always far more beneficial for us to remain agnostic about others, simply due to the fact that there is far more to that person than you can conceptualize or see right now. Just like there is more to you than anyone else can see. Trust this so you can free your mind of the burden of having to constantly defend a reality that no one else is participating.

Just like we don't realize that someone else isn't the picture that we've projected on to them, we should also realize that our mind is far too finite to always understand the complexities that are happening underneath our own hood. You couldn't possibly comprehend all that you are which makes finding your true identity impossible in this life. This isn't a problem as much as an adventure of self-discovery that lasts as long as we do. If you were to "arrive", you'd find yourself thoroughly bored with your life. Sometimes we have strong emotions about something or someone which makes it relatively easy to discern whether we like them or not, but even those feelings are subject to deep human flaw. For example, you might not like someone and your mind could easily confabulate a reason for the adverse feelings to protect yourself from what's really going on. What is possible is that the person you don't like might phrase something in a way that triggers a pain point that your father caused two decades ago. Since you never acknowledged it, the pain remains outside of your awareness, only popping up to control your reality from behind the scenes. You still know how you feel about that pain, but perhaps if you knew why you felt what you felt, you'd be far less likely to entertain the adverse emotion. "Oh, this is representative of something far deeper than my relationship with this person," is dealt with differently than "Whoa, this person is making it their life's work to make me miserable or mad." That's rarely anyone's life's work. We just have to stop acting like it is if we want to change that particular narrative.

Unfortunately, until we take the time to sit with what has hurt us and what has programmed us in the past, we will remain a slave to that thing. What you consciously perceive is often interpreted by a host of psychological mechanisms that, ironically enough, you aren't even aware. In some sense, it has to be this way. Many researchers have found that at any given moment, our senses are perceiving roughly eleven million bit of information per second. For this reason, our brains have put in place selective processes to cope with it all, and make the best decisions for survival based on the information that has been received. Right now, as you are reading this, you are hearing sounds in the distance. You are feeling the temperature against your skin. Your proprioception is keeping track of where you are in time and space. Yet, you are mostly focused on reading and comprehending the information in this book. If we didn't have unconscious processing systems we would be constantly overwhelmed and we would find it difficult to actually act in the world.

Aside from opening up a conversation about deep, hidden sexual fantasy, one of Sigmund Freud's greatest contributions to humanity was his large body of work dealing with the unconscious mind. Before his work, behavioral scientists had trouble conceptualizing how you could possibly be controlled by or even act on an awareness that ran counter to your own. Now we take this knowledge for granted, but it is difficult to imagine how anyone would go about trying to change their behavior without being aware of the intense drive that pushes that behavior from behind the scenes. Most likely, you have come up against this same drive. When you want something outwardly, yet your subconscious is aligned for something else, attaining that thing will feel impossible. Cue the millions of people that outwardly want to make millions of dollars but can't seem to do it, despite having the knowledge about what it is that they need to do. The problem occurs deeper than the level of knowing. The problem occurs because you have not embodied what it is that you actually do know. Information without alignment of action is potential that will never be met.

When it comes to acting in the world by your own volition, the ability to align the subconscious drives with the conscious mind is imperative. In order to do that, we must first look with what we are dealing, how it works, and where we can best focus our energy in making it work for us instead of against us. We have to acknowledge the biological drive for survival simply because people throughout history who failed to acknowledge it in large part, never passed on their DNA. This means that they technically, aren't like you. The price of being here is that you have to contend with the evolution that made it possible.

You might note that at any point when I am referencing your different sub personalities and unconscious motivations, I am talking about them like they are separate from you. This is because they are. You are not your limited belief system that are stopping you from making money or getting in a good relationship or even your thoughts about those things. You are simply experiencing them. This is key to our understanding if we are ever going to be able to start changing these beliefs. Just simple awareness can make a drastic difference in what we allow to rule our lives.

As we further examine the way that our subconscious acts on our behalf, we have to recognize that the patterns it acts on are just a catalyst for action. The thing that makes the subconscious particularly effective is that it actually has feelings associated with its beliefs. This is why overcoming it is so difficult. In some instances, these feelings offer a great deal of functionality. A gut feeling, for example, is often the result of your subconscious detecting risk in a given situation and it is trying to notify you of the issue. There is a rift between the patterns you have observed and whatever you are observing. This speaks further to the complexities of your inner processing systems as they retain the ability to accurately perceive risk and calculate the odds of a risk in a split second.

This function which appears to be automatic, does cause concern however. The quicker a reaction might be, the higher the chance of an associated error in that decision. While it's typically in your best interest to listen to a "gut feeling", doing so correctly is a learned habit. Sometimes we feel awful about a situation but haven't developed the ability to listen to our intuition and as a result, we don't connect what we're feeling with the right thing that's happening around us. We still marry the person, or take the job, or do the action, even amidst low level dissonance about the decision.

The "gut feeling" is the best manifestation of the subconscious. It helps us figure out how to be in the world by giving us little nudges, should we decide to learn how to listen to it. At its worst it tells you to be scared in times of change, or angry in times of turmoil. Feelings, are turned into emotions when you add a thought to them and they will only get in your way if you aren't in control of them. This is often the result because of the inability of the subconscious to plan for the future and conceptualize your situation in the broad scheme of your life. You feel fear from change, your mind adds a narrative to it in order to keep you alive which may or may not be correct, and next thing you know you have an emotion about change that is unhelpful.

It's a challenging thing to sift through your own humanity, leveraging what you can and dispensing with what isn't serving you. One of the hardest things to do is to consider everything that you believe to be true about the world and then figure out if you actually believe that thing or if you are simply acting out of ingrained patterns. The good thing is that if you act out your beliefs fully, it won't take long to see which ones don't resonate. The part we tend to get hung up on is having the wherewithal and courage to make pattern changes when we realize that our current ones are no longer serving us or what we want for our lives.

Chapter 8

WHY SELF-ACTUALIZING LIZARDS DON'T EXIST

"Your own self-realization is the greatest service you can render the world."

— Ramana Maharshi

Much of our compulsion in life can be explained by the limbic system. This is the oldest part of our brains (also known as the brain stem) and it developed so that the majority of our species could keep natural selection from selecting us. Its job is to turn on your nervous system when you are in danger in order to alert you and give you the ability to escape said danger. This is often why, when you are presented with something that scares you, your body reacts to it far quicker than your brain can comprehend what is actually going on. This system has been aptly termed, "the lizard brain" due to the fact that this makes up a majority of lizard brain function. A lizard for example, just wants to know if they should stay or go and they aren't so concerned with being their best selves in the meantime.

Over time, one of the major contributing factors that began to separate humans from the rest of the animal kingdom was the development of new parts of our brain. The last of these developments, the prefrontal cortex, is responsible for giving us choice in what we do. It is due to the prefrontal cortex that we have the ability to actually make our decisions instead of being at the beck and call of our instincts. If you can, think back to a situation where you seemed to be triggered by something; maybe someone cut you off in traffic or maybe you were let down by a friend that flaked on plans. The best way to understand the way these two parts of your brain work is by thinking about how you felt as soon as you were triggered. The increase in heart rate, sweaty palms or forehead, your breath becoming more rapid and shallow and harder to slow down. Most likely your mind also started attaching all kinds of crazy narratives to whatever happened as you began to try to find reasons why something has happened. All of this happening is a result of your limbic system reacting to stress and then your mind doing what it does and trying to rationalize the feeling.

It's worth noting here than many of us are walking around in such a reactive state 24/7 that we rarely even notice the turning on of our sympathetic nervous system over and over throughout the day. What happens next is that the narrative that your mind is running with is then picked up by your ego. All of a sudden, whatever happened around you must have happened to you. Lots of people will get cut off in traffic and then not let it go until they can tell someone about the injustice that they've incurred. The ego will make every single thing about itself whether it is or not. The ego is why you feel the need to tell someone when things happen to you. Recognize that there is no justifiable reason to carry around everything that happens around you or to you. Much of the time, it's simply unhelpful. Whether that thing is good or bad, your life isn't going to be made better by attaching your identity to what you go through… especially when you go through something impulsively. This accounts for the emotional roller coaster that many of us are on throughout our day to day lives.

As you get a little space from the trigger, something else happens. The part of you that knows better begins to speak up and you slowly either calm yourself down or at least, hopefully don't act on whatever that first impulse told you to do. That final decision was made in the prefrontal cortex. The part of you that understands we are no longer animals is the part of you that helped you stop behaving like one.

Every impulse that you have, whether it is to be reactive to something that's happened or whether it is to be attracted to something for short term pleasure, is being guided by the limbic system. In order to get really good at allowing things (whether life events or even food cravings) to pass through you and not actually affect you, you have to become good at utilizing better judgement of the prefrontal cortex. You have to become really good at understanding when the limbic system is beginning to take off on you, so that you can calmly talk yourself through it to make sure you respond in a way that is consistent with your value system. People who seem to be really good at being human are that way because they are really good at being an evolved human. They lean into their humanity, the last of evolutions gifts and as a result, they are rewarded.

Oddly enough, we are usually far less accepting of the parts of life that refuse to evolve. If someone seems even mildly racist for example, it is not tolerated today. It doesn't matter if it was a learned behavior, acceptable from where that person came, or even if they were born into generations of racist people. To be honest, most of us were, and we would never tolerate that type of behavior. Yet, when it comes to our brain, we allow our day to be ruled by something that hasn't evolved in millions of years. In fairness, most of us are so in our ego that we don't actually understand that we even have an option, especially when our body and our day are being hijacked by our oldest operating system. It just feels like it's us and that we don't have a choice in the matter.

This is why it's so important to understand who you really are and what makes up your true identity. This is why it's important to realize that you aren't your ego, or your thoughts, or even your behaviors and characteristics. You are the one that is aware of these things. If you are aware, then you have created the opportunity for choice. If you don't, the chances are great that you will attach it to an inconsequential part of your day like a traffic jam or a sugar craving. We really have to work on living intentionally so that our legacy doesn't become the sum total of our impulses while we're here.

When you are stimulated into a response, and you choose to act differently by being aware when your limbic system is pushing you to act, you can actively choose your next evolution. You have to create space between compulsion and action, however, to get your prefrontal cortex involved. If you don't do this, you will always do what your nervous system wants you to do. Unfortunately, that is often at odds with what we actually want for ourselves or our lives. This is especially true when trying to change or recover from an addictive behavior. With addiction, what you'll find is an extreme narrowing of what excites you. Much of what we feel compelled to do also stimulates a dopamine response in our brain which is a neuro-transmitter that is released by certain activities and is responsible for feeling good in the moment. Unfortunately, that good feeling is reduced as you engage in the same activity over and over, because you are adapting to it. Over time, most addictive behaviors take more and more exposure to stimulate the desired response.

This is one of the detriments to porn in the human psyche. If you adapt to watching a "gang bang," it is likely that interaction with your partner is slowly going to stimulate you less, and create less arousal for you. Monogamy takes so much work in order to keep the spark lit, but it is so much harder when you are fighting your brain when you have taught it that it can have dopamine whenever it wants it.

Getting the life that you want is quite difficult. That difficulty is increased when we give our attention to things that derail our motivations and turn our brains into antenna, only capable of picking up on pleasure. Yet, if we engage in our lives without thinking, that is exactly what we find ourselves doing. In light of this adaptation to stimulus, you must always be vigilant in trying to discern the nature of your impulses. Just like feelings can either be harmful in your life, or a guiding hand, so too can your impulses and desires be either harmful or helpful. Discerning which is which is where the art of living is really tested.

You can want something badly and that thing can turn into your life's calling. You can also want something so badly that it turns out to be an addictive behavior that leads you further from your realized potential.

The best way to understand the nature of your behavior is to think about the feeling you get after the dopamine response wears off. If you give in to an impulse and it leaves you feeling even emptier afterward, you know you were chasing the dopaminergic pathways that will never truly satisfy. If you continue to do it, you are emboldening those pathways. Every time you do, you make it just a little bit harder to kick that habit later on. In most cases, our impulsions are actually a symptom of something else. There is usually some resistance in your life somewhere that you are trying to cover up with the compulsion to do something that makes you feel good in the moment.

Outside of simply making you feel good in the moment however, dopamine plays a role in motivation as well. It will actually drive you toward the addictive behavior. That is why it is not enough to try and resist dopamine causing activities but also that you replace that behavior with one that is more preferable to your life. When you find yourself truly in the grips of impulse, it feels like a visceral longing for that thing. You'll notice those compulsions are quite overwhelming as the neuro pathways have been perfected and cemented over the course of millions of years. In light of this, if we want to help people on a larger scale, we must stop treating them as if addiction to anything is a moral failing. As long as you make people feel bad about a compulsion that is far larger than themselves and that they don't fully understand, you will continue to forfeit the ability to solve the problem. There are neural pathways that must be rewired and repattered. Will power will play a role in that process but something that strong demands that you understand it fully.

Cutting out self destructive behavior such as self sabotage is also a matter of reprogramming. Humans learn to self soothe and make ourselves feel centered for things that make us feel out of sorts. Unfortunately, most of our self-soothing activities are also self-destructive. Many of us have learned to feel centered while in chaos because our psyche has spent so much time there, it's grown comfortable. This is why some of us seemingly go from one drama to the next wondering why it's following us. We are comfortable in the drama at a subconscious level and we are recreating it wherever we go.

In many cases, we find ourselves so driven by our compulsory systems that we act against our better judgment. We forgo our invitations to live higher and become more because we don't want to let go of the self-destructive behavior that is helping us stay centered. The truth is that most people could start living differently today, right now in fact. They just aren't ready to let go of what's kept them safe for all these years -- even if "safe" isn't serving their soul. In a very real way, we must show up for ourselves daily and remind ourselves of what we really want, so that we don't end up becoming only the sum total of our urges and compulsions which are derived from a time of which we have no recollection. Much of learning who we are and being able to have ownership over ourselves is simply understanding our deep seated desires and then doing our best to not allow them to run our lives. We must see them for what they are and learn to integrate them. When you do something that you know is bad for you and you intentionally hide it and keep it in the shadows, you empower it and make it harder to let go of.

The best way that we can continue to evolve our consciousness is to root out and make ourselves aware of all the things in our lives that are causing a compulsion in the first place. Many polytheistic cultures dramatize human motivations with the creation of different gods. Simply having an awareness of the different gods (motivations) you unconsciously serve can help in understanding why you do what you do. The truth is that we all worship a faceless deity who promises a heaven that we'll never actually taste. Our job is to find out what deity is currently taking up the most dominion within us, consequently holding our best future over us.

We unknowingly put our hope for the future in the gods we are unconsciously serving, and never realize that their only plans for us consist of the purgatory where we already exist. If you never realize this, you will continue to resolve to change, only to find yourself in the same place. Your desire for positive, self-directed evolution must overcome your desire to serve what's been comfortable up until now. Safety, comfort, sex, drama, money, fame, validation in many forms -- all of these are jealous gods in that they all demand our obedience. If you remain willingly unaware of their existence within you, they will continue to direct your behavior without you knowing how or why. We often don't like to admit that we are driven by validation or fame but as I recall, admittance is step one. You'll never change what you don't recognize.

Conceptualizing these as gods is beneficial because the pursuit of them will often force you to overrule your own values and principles if you aren't careful. The subconscious mind stimulates a thought that causes an emotional response and before you know what's happening, your thoughts create a feeling and your body will stimulate action based on what you feel. Both of these are essentially the result of programming. Each and every interaction we've been privy and that our ancestors have been privy to has found their reminisces etched on the inside of our operating manual. When we saw our dad open the door for our mom, or when we saw him hit her. When our ninth grade teacher told us we would never amount to anything, or when she told us we were the smartest student she'd ever had. Every. Single. Interaction. Notes have been etched on the back of our mind. "This is how we survive."

While there is clearly a good reason for our survival mechanisms to override all others, it is also important to recognize that offensive and defensive strategies aren't the same. You don't get rich simply by trying to not go broke. You won't be a good lover when your focus is on not getting hurt. You won't be able to live fully when all you are doing is trying not to die. You won't thrive if you allow your actions to be dictated on the basis of survival. In tough situations, it can be helpful to ask yourself if you are trying to thrive or survive? Are your current actions in line with your intended results? A little consciousness goes a long way in that respect. A survival mindset throws up walls around the heart to avoid getting hurt. A thriving mindset opens the heart further to learn more about what it needs to understand, despite the immediate or possible pain involved.

Of course we have these survival mechanisms for a reason but again, it is our discernment and our deeply human ability to choose what serves us, which will make the difference in whether or not we are happy with our lives. When you are walking in the woods, it is better to believe that a dangling tree branch could be a snake than assume that a snake is a dangling tree branch. In this case our limbic systems reaction to flee before we have a conscious thought is desired. When your lover seems distant, the survival mechanism to protect your ego and flee might be to your detriment. The fact is that the life you want is going to come with risk, and the strong possibility for failure. We shouldn't allow our failure to be confused with not surviving, as it is actually necessary to thrive.

If we are to live our lives as we are currently, allowing the limbic system and the subconscious to direct our decisions out of fear, our chance at a happy and successful life is solely left up to the world for which we have been conditioned. We are a product of our environment in the truest sense. Knowing when to go against your own need for survival is an art in and of itself. When you transcend survival mode and you begin to thrive, you are positioned to feel the depth in life. People who dislike their life are assuredly living out of scarcity, lack and the need to simply survive. It is when we begin to make decisions by our own volition that we cultivate passion, love, and bring joy back into our lives. Passion, joy, and love are all decisions that we have to make. You have to consciously cultivate these things in your life if you actually want them.

When our lover gives us the sense that they are trying to protect themselves, or that they have walls up, your compulsions are going to tell you that you must also put up walls. It then becomes an arms race and no longer has the space to be a loving relationship. As cliché as it may seem, love is the only thing that can transcend the walls we erect. What I know to be true is that you aren't looking for an enemy in a partner. A thriving mindset says that it is you two against the problem, not each other. If you decide to choose love and meet their defense with offensive strategies, one of two things will happen. You will either break down his defense and allow space for real connection to occur, or you will understand that you have done all that you can do. We have to meet people where they are in life. Eventually, if we realize that the people in our lives aren't trying to go to the same place that we are, we need to be at peace with a diversion of paths.

Our need for survival also tends to remind us of all of the scariest outcomes of our decisions, as it has been specifically attuned to be sensitive to negative situations. Which makes perfect sense if your chief concern is survival. For those of us who are looking to build a life of meaning, we must stop the narrative in our head that is focusing on the negative out of survival. In life we largely go where we put our attention, so one can easily draw a logical conclusion as to where a survival mindset gets us. You can spend all of your time (in fact you probably do) thinking about what you don't want. "I don't want to go broke," "I don't want to be alone," etc.... Instead, you can put your focus on what you do want and choose to believe that there is more available to you. You can think about how much you do want to earn, and you can work on yourself intently believing that when the universe does put someone in your path, that you will be the best version of you for that person that you possibly could be.

The second mode of being, cultivating a creation mindset, ensures that you evolve past the trappings that have kept you in negative situations in the past. It just requires considerably more effort because awareness can be exhausting. Anyone who has walked through the woods for an extended period of time at night can attest to this fact. It uses mental bandwidth and resources in order to stay tuned in and focused. When you first start cultivating awareness, this is what it feels like. Over time, you learn to be relaxed, yet aware and focused, another of the artistic endeavors involved with being human.

Both of these mindsets are available to you but both will get you very different outcomes, as they are clearly very different conversations. "I'm afraid to go broke if I go on my own," is a much different conversation than, "I want to make six figures with my own business." It shifts the focus and therefore the subsequent actions and results to solutions instead of problems. If we want to thrive, we have to learn to be solution-oriented. The narrative that you choose to follow will lead to very different outcomes. Words matter. Your internal monologue matters. Your disposition matters. It all matters.

Understand that you aren't obligated to spend the next five to six decades at the mercy of narratives that see you always accepting and never challenging. You have evolved into a creature that challenges and eventually, changes. At our best, we aren't scared of divergent thinking, we celebrate it. We continue to push our species forward because of the renegades that choose to reject a narrative that sees them as a victim of circumstance or biology or anything else. The presumption of being a renegade is that you fully understand what you are up against. If you understand the underlying system at work, you stand a chance at changing it.

Chapter 9

TECHNOLOGY AND CHOICE

"It has become appallingly obvious that our
technology has exceeded our humanity."

— Albert Einstein

Our world has evolved and become industrialized at an extremely rapid
rate. Rampant consumerism driven by competitive capitalistic markets
were shifted into overdrive by the advancement of technology in the late
twentieth century, effectively giving birth to the age of information. As a
result, the entire world of thought has become available to the masses at
the touch of a button. This age of information has created incredible
opportunities for good in the human race. We can now spread ideas glob-
ally. Education has become accessible, regardless of where you are from, so
long as you have an antenna capable of receiving it. According to statista.
com, 42.63% of people on the planet today have a smartphone.

Life changing information is pushed into the airwaves at every
moment, which decentralizes power, reduces barriers to entry for most
things (specifically professions), and gives upward mobility to people that
previously had none. You would be hard pressed to find a historian that
doesn't believe this is the best time to have ever lived with regards to

prosperity, opportunity, and choice. The rising technological tide truly is lifting ships that had been dry docked since the beginning of time.

We now have more choices than ever before regarding how to conduct our lives. We used to have one or two stores to choose from to buy most things in the United States. Now you have every store that could possibly exist, and they are all in your pocket regardless of which country you reside. For all of the good that this brings us, it also brings with it a downside. People like to say "first word problems" as a sarcastic remark about having to deal with something petty, but the truth is that first world problems are real problems. The people that dismiss them and don't work through them typically end up suffering from the rising first world depression rate. Since the first world leads the rest of the world, we have a very real responsibility to inspect the variables that we are introducing into society, and ensure we are on the right track. It is hard to believe how an increasingly stressed out and depressed society could lead the world anywhere worth being if we don't learn from what's not working.

Nothing in this life that is good can exist without the opposite also existing. God has his Devil. If you don't give the Devil his due, you will find yourself lost in the underworld rather quickly. One of the shadows we are seeing from our expansion in opportunity is indecision. We don't travel down this road of life very long, so spending a few decades at a fork can turn into a rather large problem. When there is only one path to walk down, it's only a problem if you don't want to go that way. When there are unlimited paths to walk down that all seem enticing, it is a problem because there is only one of you. Our problems are changing but they aren't going away.

The basic human decision is made as an aggregate of the information one has been privy to up until that point. We have grown incredibly good at finding the necessary information and using it to change our own lives, so long as we don't allow emotion to make the decision for us, and the information we gather is actually pertinent. In many cases, we incorrectly weigh the information that we have because we don't understand our own value system. This is often the result we get when the pressure we are receiving from the world around us is at odds with our internal value system and we don't know it. We just feel stuck, and even though the decisions look good on paper. Something within us, far deeper than paper, is pleading with us not to go that way. Most likely this is a force that you've experienced in your own life. You feel stuck or in a rut and because nothing is actually keeping you stuck, you feel frustrated and at a loss as to why.

Much of the time that we feel stuck in life, when we can't figure out where it all went wrong, we can trace the feeling back to an opportunity that was too good to pass up. Accepting your life, such as what happens when someone gives you something that's too good to pass up, is a defensive play. Regardless of what the opportunity is, the person that says, "I have to take this because," is no longer playing offense in their own lives. She went from creating to accepting, and when you accept without taking the time to see if the opportunity is something that you would create, you don't quite know where you are going to end up. You have to be in the driver's seat if you want to be the one that gets to decide where you are headed.

The way that you look at the world is through your specific set of values. The reason that we all get along is because, for the most part, we have overlapping values. To some degree, most of us value things like honesty, courage, and integrity as examples. Understand that these aren't just what you like about life or other people. These affect the way you look at the world. As a consequence, you make major decisions based off of it.

If a soldier gives his life in service to his country, for example, that can only take place because he values country or nationality over self. You don't get to that end state any other way, except through value or accident. Knowing this can be immensely valuable. If you look at this decision with reverence, it is because your value system is set up in a similar manner. If you look at such a thing with pity or disdain, your value system is set up differently. You can see with this analogy that we are all living in different worlds based on our value system. This is why you and another person can live in the same city and one of you thinks it is amazing and full of opportunity while the other thinks it is too expensive and stifling. Although you are in the same place physically, you are living in different worlds based on your own intrinsic value system.

We know that if you have a decision to make, because values are the substructure of your life, if you pivot toward them, you will always incur a sense of meaning in what you are doing. Often our "good opportunities" don't line up completely with our value set. As a result, we have chosen what looks good on paper over what feels good in the heart. Over time, this betrayal of self only grows more pronounced as we resonate less and less with the world around us. This is because we all have a basic expectation that our internal needs for satisfaction in life will be met. When they aren't met, things begin to unravel as we view our good opportunities with resentment.

Resentment that we don't work through will eventually tear us apart. It manifests in two distinct ways depending on your personality. It will grow into hatred or apathy, both will create turmoil in the soul if they are allowed to continue for too long. The moment you notice resentment building in your life, you have been given an invitation to change. Your brain has shown you that something in your life isn't working and you need something else. If you don't accept that invitation, you will find yourself sinking deeper and deeper into the rut.

What often happens when someone finally realizes he's ready for change is that he bounces this desire off of all of his old programming. Everything and everyone that has taught us what we should do, what we should prioritize, and what we should accept. The implications of these things have created walls in our thinking and we have a ton of trouble getting past them or seeing them as false. This is when the real party begins. The human psyche now begins to spiral downward as it can't conceive of a way to get past these walls. It knows it is at odds with the world and because value systems are so deeply ingrained, we feel as though we are destined to never get the life that we want.

Maybe we believe we have invested too much time in our relationship or our job and we are feeling like we've come too far to make any kind of drastic change. In this moment, it feels like our world has trapped us when in reality it is only our thinking. When you are stuck or in a rut, you are stuck between your soul saying, "I know I was meant for more," and your head, which has been deeply conditioned by the world around you, telling you that you weren't. The truth is that you were. Everything around us is unknown and so we have built into our psyche the ability to deal with it. In fact, we have an entire hemisphere of the brain which is specifically adapted for contending with the unknown. This is the right side that is often associated with creativity. Think about it this way -- part of you was built to understand order (that's the analytical left side of the brain), but part of you was born to understand chaos, i.e. to take abstract notions and make something out of them. You were built to withstand major pivots but conditioned not to.

All of this goes to show the continued importance in how we value the information we are curating. Namely, we need to determine whether or not the information we curate actually speaks to our values or not. If you always pivot toward your value set, you'll never feel completely wrong. Typically, we're always hoping for just a little more information before we make any major decisions. It is only when we are convinced we know enough do we execute on our intentions, based on the opportunities that we've created. Fundamentally, that's how we've crafted our entire world. We've gathered information and executed over and over with varying degrees of success. This explains in part why we have a tendency to want to simplify everything in our world. It is our finite minds that grasp at information for a sense of understanding with the hopes of control. Yet, it is possible that in our oversimplification, we gather information that is unhelpful.

This entire life is a paradox. You have the capacity to hold space for multiple things at one time and in doing so, you get a much more accurate understanding of your life. You thinking that you have to decide on one path over another right now, or thinking that you can only feel one thing at a time is causing far more pain than any one path or any one feeling possibly could. It seems like everywhere you look there are people lining up to take sides on one issue or another. The goal of this tribalism is to give people a sense of belonging, which helps them feel safe. The often unnoticed side effect is that it creates further division between tribes which over the course of a long life, is actually worse for the tribes involved. This is the danger when you take a hard stance on a complex issue.

Due to where you and I fall in history, technology itself is one of the things on which we seem to feel the need to take sides. People everywhere want to either vilify technology or praise it. What people are failing to recognize is that humans have always relied heavily on our tools to assist us with living our lives. Furthermore, tools are neither good nor bad but an extension of what is good or bad in the people that use them. It is the intention behind the swing of a hammer that gives it aim and makes it either a destructive act or a helpful one. The same iPhone can be used to donate to charity or plan a large scale terrorist attack. With all great tools of power comes the responsibility to wield them correctly. When Shakespeare wrote the lines for Hamlet to say, "Nothing is good nor bad but it is thinking that makes it so, " he articulated a correct standpoint toward technology, years before it would exist.

Barry Schwartz in his paper, "Can There Ever Be Too Many Flowers Blooming?" goes into great detail about how badly all of our options these days actually tend to make us feel. While some choice is good, he argues, there is a point where you reach the law of diminishing returns. In essence, every time you are given an option, you increase the chances that you will grow less content with the choices that you do make. He writes, "The logic behind the presumption that if some choice is good, more choice is better seems compelling. But what might be called the "psychology" of choice tells us something different. In the last decade, research evidence has accumulated that there can be too much of a good thing—that a point can be reached at which options paralyze rather than liberate. And when there are too many choices, two different things happen. First, satisfaction with whatever is chosen diminishes. And second, people choose not to choose at all."

Everyday billions of people are trying to figure out what to do with their lives. They are surveying the options and trying to find a direction that they'll be happy with. A 2015 census study revealed that there are currently 23,887 universities for higher education in the world. Imagine how many programs in total there are between the tens of thousands of schools that offer them? We are having people at eighteen years of age make the decision of what to do with the rest of their lives between the twenty three thousand options. Now consider the fact that you were one of those people. If you are starting to feel dissonance in your life, and struggling to find out why, perhaps it is because your well-being has been at the mercy of a process that you don't fully understand.

As Shwartz points out in his *TedTalk*, when you order food at a restaurant, you can be completely content... until your friend orders something that looks better. Now you've taken away a bit of your own satisfaction just with the knowledge that other things exist. Consider the fact that we are doing that with every option in our life including where to work, where to live, and who to date. All of the options are great, right up until they're not.

What's more, thinking back to how people find themselves in a rut, you see that society has stigmatized a pivot later in life. People in their thirties, forties, and fifties fret about starting over because we're made to believe that when we leave something, that we are starting back at zero. Understand that is never true. You always bring with you, who you've become in the process of doing what you've done. That is a social construct that we hold ourselves to at the peril of our own happiness. The truth is that you are always free to move and to shift, and realistically, you should. Until you find "the thing," you'll always wonder if it's the right thing. If you feel like you haven't found the right thing yet, it's because you haven't. Sometimes, the thing is good for a time but as values are changed and realized, so to is our need to meet those values.

Due to the fact that we know choice makes us less happy, and because we have more choices than we ever have, is it that hard to see why we are all searching for more happiness? What we really need in life is a "yes" so strong that everything else becomes a stronger "no". You don't have time to say no to seven billion people, but when you start dating just one person you love, that is exactly what you are doing. How might we apply that to every other facet of our lives? This is why we must prioritize finding the soul's path. Until the deepest you recognizes the way that they want to spend their lives, the human side will flail in confusion. As we've seen time and again, the first thing that most people do when they want to find answers is to look outward. They research programs, categorize them by interest, prerequisites, price, or whatever else they deem as important. While rationale should certainly play a part in the decision making promise, we almost never stop amidst all of the chaos and just ask ourselves what it is that we actually want.

In essence, we end up wanting to be the CEO without asking ourselves if we really want the day to day pressure of managing lots of people and making critical decisions about the well-being of an organization. What sounds good might not be what is good for you, and while asking yourself what you really want might seem like an obvious first step, we almost never actually utilize it. Instead we have conversations about it with people we trust or like and we think about it in passing. The inherent problem is that whenever we are in passing, we aren't capable of thinking clearly enough. We are essentially too busy constantly consuming that there is no room in our minds for authenticity to be expressed or thought. We have reached a point where the processing power of the human mind is being inundated with inputs. According to redcrowmarketing.com "Digital Marketing experts estimate that most Americans are exposed to around 4,000 to 10,000 advertisements each day." Indeed, in just reading that study online, I took the time to count twenty-two ads on the webpage, all vying for my bandwidth just like they are the server that is hosting them. This presents a real issue when your contentment in life is largely determined by what you think of the things that are going on in your life. This is especially detrimental when you don't have the ability to actually think clearly about the things that are going on in your life. It might feel like you are able to block these inputs out mentally, but as we'll see later, this is just to spare your conscious self from feeling inundated.

In the back of your mind there is a room with clutter all over the place. There's a desk with papers strewn about that contain every piece of information that you've ever learned and there are people you don't even remember meeting, all milling about, taking up a small piece of band-width. The secretary that runs the back room is feeding information to your executive function as it thinks you need it to keep you alive but their job is getting more and more difficult to maintain with all that you are allowing into the back room. Every time you're in conversation and something is on the "tip of your tongue," the secretary is rifling through papers with everything you've ever learned on them and frantically searching for the right concept or word for which you are looking. You can imagine that as you go through your life, with everything that gets stacked back there, the process gets slowed down a bit. In order to compete with all that information, the secretary is forced to prioritize based on need.

Since what you need more than anything is to keep living, survival is placed at the top of the hierarchy just like it is with every other aspect of your psyche. If you are in a crowded room and you somehow hear your name amidst the others, the secretary that's processing the incoming information lets you know immediately that there's something which might pertain to you happening across the room. This is why you can be a crowded room at a party and hear your name and immediately pull it out of the ruckus. You also won't be able to ignore it without at least looking over to see why your name was brought up.

At times we'll get a momentary thought that is immediately lost to incoming information. While we don't have a way of measuring how many times per day we all say, "I forgot what I was going to say," it doesn't seem like a stretch based on experience and context to guess that the number is rising dramatically. With all of the information you are constantly sifting through, how could you possibly know which thoughts are yours and which have been placed by clever marketers? Rarely do we take the time to actually go into that back room ourselves and start organizing it all. Instead we become directed by the secretary. He hands us information and we immediately course correct our actions to adjust. When you start meditating regularly, you actually gain the ability to sit with the secretary and analyze the information instead of quickly reacting to everything that's shoved in your face, which may or may not be important to your overall well-being.

As we look to pick our path in life, what we inevitably find is that we have a wide availability of options that can wreak havoc on our psyche. As finite beings we can only process and decide so quickly. Often we find ourselves relying on physiological reactions to direct our response instead of rational decision making. In western culture we tend to meet more options with more consumption. Reasoning to ourselves that if some is good, more must be better. The person that prioritizes quantity over quality however, is likely to find that each task takes them further from a meaningful life. You can't busy yourself in lieu of knowing what to do. Despite the fact that most of us keep trying to.

Some of the inputs that we all must wade through while trying to find a meaningful direction for our lives is navigating all that we're told we "should do." Our parents, teachers, preachers and friends all have different ideas about what would be best for our lives or what a successful life should look like in the first place. The truest sign of adulthood is coming to grips with the fact that none of these people have answers for your life that are better than your own.

You just have to learn to trust yourself. You've been given intuition for feeling the right answer just like you've been given the ability to apply reason to your options. Others will be able to apply reason to your life but they can't feel it and because of this they'll never know what's truly right for you. The magic in this life is found once you begin to get past the programming and the expectations that your life has saddled on you. We all have a million things we could do or feel like we should do. The secret is that once you begin to trust your thoughts and you get a clearer picture of what you really want to be doing, it turns out to be the thing that you should be doing.

One of the little known facts about our universe is that once you are aligned and doing what you should and want to be doing, the universe feels as though it is conspiring to help you in that thing. This isn't to be confused with manifestation practices such as that which is outlined in the book, *The Secret*. This is a well-documented matter of fact. You will go where you focus and you will see the doors that are open to you that you might not have otherwise seen if you weren't focused in the right place. When you begin to see options for what you want unfolding, you have brought your attention to something you want. The term for this is the *Baader-Meinhof* phenomenon. It is a cognitive process known as selective attention. When you are struck by a new word or concept or idea, you begin to unconsciously keep an eye out for that thing. It's why when you buy a new car, you suddenly notice so many of the same model on the road.

When you are on the right path in life and you have a picture of that path, there is an alignment that takes place between you conscious and subconscious mind. The significance here is that when both parts of you are on board with the direction, the opportunities "seem" to present themselves. The reality is that without this alignment, you just wouldn't be aware of them. It is not that the right path is easier, it's just that you'll feel more at ease in pursuing it as you don't struggle as much to see the next move.

This alignment takes lots of reprogramming to fully acquire, but it must start with an authentic call to adventure and the willingness to say no to what isn't that. It is not something you simply pursue because it seems easy or because it's available. Everyone has good ideas for the next great business. Anyone has the ability to write their first few thoughts down in their memoir. It is the middle that will test your allegiance to your ideals. When everything gets tough and the struggle sets in and the easiest thing to do in the world becomes to start the next thing or to pacify yourself with an inconsequential thing, that is when your commitment matters. That's when it will have mattered whether you took the initial right first step or not. In light of our overwhelming chance of taking the wrong path, the question then becomes, "How do we find the path that will actually meet those needs?" As it turns out, you've actually known all along. At least at one point you did. You just lost the ability to listen to the voice that was offering all of the hints.

If you've lost creativity or direction in your life, then unplugging might be the thing that allows you to get back in touch with the voice that's been there all along. What you'll find is that deep down you know exactly who you want to be in the world, you just have to reach the point where you are comfortable listening to and trusting that voice. When it comes to finding meaning and crafting a life that actually feels like your life, you have to learn that nothing outside of you is more important that what is inside of you. You have to learn to elevate the mundane thoughts and desires that you have for your life because you can never be sure of where following those thoughts might lead. You have to trust in the fact that you are given desires, passions and interests for a reason and to ignore those comes at the peril of who you were meant to be. It is a slap in the face to the cosmos to worry about whether or not you are good enough for someone or something else, when you could be crafting the unique gift that you have for the world.

Everyone that has built their life into exactly what they want it to be understands that there are no coincidences, seemingly random recurring desires without meaning, or ideas for what you could do, that pop into your head that don't matter. They have listened to themselves and followed leads. Often against the advice of others. If at any point you prioritize your own intuition over another's opinion, you've taken the first step toward authenticity. Ironically, the only way to fully be of service to others, is to actually take this step and prioritize yourself. Many people will spend their lives as "people pleasers," without ever realizing the injustice they are doing to the world around them. There is no nobility in sacrificing who you are and what you want for others because in that moment you are making the decision to hoard your gifts. If you never step into the full expression of yourself, you'll never know what you could truly offer the world. Instead of doing the things you want to do, you will see that your schedule is hijacked by the emergencies of others at every corner. It will be increasingly difficult to know what you actually want because your life will be the result of end-lessly catering to the desires of others.

We are all exposed, every day, to people that expect things from us; things we should do, things we have to do, and usually these are things we don't want to do but do anyway based on some misguided sense of respon-sibility or obligation. Have you ever said "no" to someone? Have you ever said "no" to someone or something and then realized you were immediately filled with self-doubt? Have you ever instantly followed said no by backing off or engaging in ten minutes of word vomit as you try to justify yourself? It takes a deep understanding of who you really are, what you really want and most importantly what you're really worth in order to stand firmly on a no. The difference is that once you are able to stand behind your decisions with conviction, the choices that you make become extremely valuable to you. At first, saying no to someone can feel very personal, like it is an attack on who they are. As you let go of all the alternatives for your life and narrow in on what you truly want, those decisions become much more black and white. Does this or does this not get you closer to where you want to be? Are your values being met or not? Anything beyond that is secondary in the decision making process if you want your life to incur meaning.

This might all sound foreign if you've fallen into the trap of expectations and people pleasing, but regardless of whether or not you recognize it, you are worth your own time. You might not believe it now but that lack of awareness almost always stems from the fact that you haven't yet figured out exactly who you are. You are still operating on what you should do and who you think you should be and the disconnect is causing you a lot of misguided emotions. It may be that you wonder why you're different than others or why people don't ever quite seem to understand you. This is nothing more than a side effect of trying to keep the real you from the world because you believe it won't be accepted. You think you need the facade to keep up appearances and be someone that others will be proud of and accept. You don't. All of those things that make you different are exactly what you can capitalize on when you find alignment and authenticity in your life. You have something to offer the world and the world needs it. But first, the world needs you to put boundaries around your time and emotions so that you can foster those inante gifts. Your experiences, no matter how good or bad they've been up until now, have uniquely positioned you to bring something into the world that only you can do in a way that only you can do it.

In order to do that however, you have to know yourself first so that you can figure out what that thing is. It might be a creative pursuit, it might be a business, it might be a child, it might be a deeper friendship or connection, its hard telling what someone else will need. And to be honest, your job isn't necessarily to decide what those things are. Your job is to figure out and do exactly what you feel called to do. The universe will work the rest out and answers will be revealed as you're ready for them.

This calls for an extreme act of faith which can be unsettling for some. For now, you will have to prioritize yourself with the faith that the path will become known as you walk down it. If you don't, you will be robbing the world of the authentic you and that "you" might be poised to do something great. Define yourself first, right here, right now, before going into the world. Spend time learning to both speak to and listen to yourself, before taking on another project, hobby, career or passion. Do this, before saying yes to anything else.

What would your life look like if you never allowed another "what if" to go unattended to? The answer is that neither you nor I have any idea. You never know when one thing will lead to another, which will help you meet someone who will introduce you to someone else who will change your life ten years down the road. The world is always unfolding in front of us and because of that, there isn't a thing that happens which you, with your finite processing power, could conclude is insignificant.

The universe is inviting you to come and be the best version of yourself through your daily interactions and thoughts. That hobby you've always wanted to try, that business that you've always wanted to start, that place you've always wanted to visit, and that person that you've always wanted to talk to. Every single one of these things could be your unique call to adventure. The person that you could be is waiting for the person that you are you to answer the call. Be vigilant in protecting your mind and not allowing it to craft a narrative that puts a wall of fear in between you and the things that you want to do with your life.

Chapter 10

THE ADVENTURER WITHIN

"A man who as a physical being is always turned toward the outside, thinking that his happiness lies outside of him, finally turns inward and discovers that the source is within him."

— Soren Kierkegaard

There are two ways that people identify dysfunction in their lives. They either look out into the world for what's wrong, or they turn inward to try and find it within themselves. The problem with looking outward for an answer is that whenever you identify something that's wrong, there is very little that you can do about it. Changing the world to find inner peace is a process that you don't have the enough time to invest. It is a matter of perspective. If the problem is you, at least you can do something about it. By looking for solutions within ourselves, we set ourselves up to exist in the world in a different way. This in turn begins to change the world that we are living in.

The danger that victimhood creates in your personality is that it gives away any power that you have to affect change. If you can keep your attention inward, what you'll find is that the world around you will react accordingly. How you feel about what is outside of you is only a reflection of what's happening inside. This is why you can only love another to the degree that you love yourself. When you look outside to the world, most of what you see is only your reflection being mirrored back to you in different forms. If you find that you are consistently re-living the same negative situations with different people, what's actually happening is that you have a dysfunction within yourself that you haven't addressed.

When you set out to modify your own behavior, you're putting your efforts where they will be effective and you'll come to understand that the outside world will follow suit. Whatever you deeply believe about the world is what will come to be true in your own life. It takes a fair amount of life before someone figures out that they are truly at the behest of their own thoughts.

This is one of the reasons that a true gratitude practice is such a potent way to change your life. By focusing on what you have to be thankful for, you shift your focus from what isn't right to what is. You then give yourself the gift of living in a world where things are right. You are going to be living in the same world either way so why not stand from a place with a better view?

For most of our early years it feels a lot more like we're victims of circumstance and that we're simply doing our best to operate within the confines of reality. The fully awake person knows that she is the one creating that reality in the first place. When you become aware of this fact, you become aware of the necessity of finding your own answers.

When we become sufficiently sick of ourselves or the life that our ego has created, we tend to reach a point where we decide that we can no longer go on in the current manner. We realize that something has to change, we just don't usually know what, so we begin our search. Typically, we respond ironically by trying to lose ourselves in the world. We make drastic changes in our appearance and we go on trips to "find ourselves." While the shift in perspective gained from a new spot on the map can be beneficial, what one inevitably finds is that her search will never turn over the answers she is looking for. Regardless of how far they travel or where they go, when the dust finally settles, they will still be the same old them that started running all that time ago. This mode of existential problem solving is rendered ineffective by the fact that you cannot possibly escape yourself while simultaneously finding yourself.

The process of finding oneself is ineffective because you are already here. Acting as if you can be found has a tendency to set us up to look outward in our search. "If we can just be in the right place, we reason, all of our troubles will go away." Instead, we should strive to know ourselves so that we can give ourselves whatever it is that we need, where it is that we find ourselves. Most of our dysfunction occurs because we only know the character that we've been playing for the world - the persona of who we believed we had to be.

Knowing oneself is not about creating the new, but rather it is about dredging up the forgotten and working through the ignored. You, in the truest sense of who you are, have been buried under the chaotic world around you. For this reason, you will do all of this growth work only to find that you've spent a significant portion of your adult life simply trying to get back to who you were as a kid. This is not just recapturing our sense of wonder or imagination, but realizing that way back then, even with our small amount of knowledge about ourselves, the world hadn't yet made us believe that we had to be someone else in order to be worthy of love or affection. We hadn't been ridiculed for not playing our role properly. If nothing else, who we were in those early years was at least an authentic expression of who we were at the time. The way that you currently show up in the world is dictated by the way that you interpret the expectations of your environment. If your ego made the judgement that your deepest desires are at odds with what right living should be, you will back-handedly sabotage every attempt at authenticity that you make. What's happening here at a subconscious level is that you are seeing yourself as someone that isn't living right and therefore doesn't deserve the things that you want.

Remember that our idea of right living is often associated with what we've been conditioned to believe. The problem is that to think there's a right way of living is an illusion propagated by people who are too scared to go out and find their own answers or too scared to engage with people that are far different from them. The expectations you have of what "right living" looks like have been put on you by the world and they are actually no more than the story that you're telling yourself about what you have noticed so far.

There is a difference between being socially adjusted and conforming to the point of no longer knowing who you are. What most people miss is that you can be well-adjusted socially and still stand on your own truths and pursue your own path. You won't lose friends or connections that matter because you realize your soul is being called to live differently. If you believe you must choose between belonging and authenticity you are holding on to a story to keep yourself from really going after what you want, or you holding on to people who aren't serving you anyway. To think that those ideologies are competing is a gross oversimplification of the human psyche. We have finite minds but they are plenty capable of maneuvering through what it is that we want while still coming into harmony with our environment. Give yourself the gift of understanding that, and you'll start truly feeling as though your direction in life has intrinsic meaning to you.

People have so much trouble finding their own identity and understanding exactly who they are because of the dynamic nature of the self. The paradoxical nature of our being is felt when you realize that you must be in touch with the eternal and unchanging self (your soul or essence), yet you are also in constant flux, as the version of you that shows up in the physical world is always making slight modifications based on the environment you're in. Our challenge is in allowing our essence to shine through despite the perceived tyranny of the environment around us.

The deeper we get into self, the more ease we feel when we're in the world. If you can remember that you are the one playing the game, but you aren't necessarily the character you're playing, you can hold space for the fact that your character will evolve and change throughout the course of your life and that's ok. As you make contact with your environment, you come to understand that each different landscape demands that you act out different aspects of your personality. This is a problem if you've been taught to deny parts of who you are because when you do, you are limiting your own tools for interacting with the world. The anger you have learned to repress might be useful if you find yourself coming up against injustice. We ironically try to be a more complete human by cutting of the parts of ourselves that we don't think serve us and in doing so, end up having to meet the world around us with an incomplete tool set.

You'll most likely have many identities as you move through the world. If you play football and also work as an executive assistant, then you most likely have to lean into different parts of who you are to be successful in each of these environments. The way to truly be at peace with the different versions of you is to allow the unchanging self, the one that's playing the game in the first place, to shine through in each thing that you do. If you have a strong soul that is comfortable leading others, perhaps that is manifested as you being both the captain of your team as well as the go-to person in the office to make things happen. You can still be more aggressive on the field and at the same time more refined in the office because that's what each social situation demands of you while still allowing your essence to shine through. Authenticity is found when essence is manifested through nuance.

Very few people in this life actually take the time to travel inward due to the pain that growth incurs. Growth is a buzz word at the moment but it will die off just as quickly as it came as people take stalk of the actual work required behind true growth. The journey into authenticity will kill you a thousand times over as you sift through what you've known and separate that from what you now know. You will realize that not all of your beliefs are serving you and you will have to dispense with some of them if you want to get to the next level in your understanding of yourself and your life. You will also realize, as your consciousness expands, that the programming which you grew up with might be too narrow to hold your new beliefs. It will be emotionally painful as your beliefs clash with your new-found knowledge and for that reason, many people find it far easier to abandon the pursuit of self and buy a new sports car to help them cope with the painful confusion about their identity. Unfortunately, the pain born of confusion will slowly make itself known as the new car smell fades.

It is through answering our call to adventure that our lives adopt a cycle of death and rebirth as the ego dies over and over in the underworld so that we can create the new within the one life that we have. By answering whatever you are called to, you will be subjected to lessons and those lessons, although painful, will teach you who you need to be in order to continue. The less ego death that you suffer in this life, the more stagnant you will become. In committing to the process of growth through the death of our outermost self, we keep ourselves on top of the turbulent waters that always sit below the surface of our lives. The turbulence is caused by the many changes and transitions to which we are always subjected. When we answer our authentic call to adventure, it gives us a forward trajectory that makes it much easier to stay above the whimsical shifting currents below us. Traditionally we wrap our identity up in what we are up to at the time and because we resist change we have a tendency to want to hold onto that identity even when it's no longer possible. In part this speaks to the problem that professionals have when transitioning to a new career. They have invested so much time and effort in their outer self (the way that the world recognizes them), they feel as if they can't let it go.

Even when we know something is over, we often hold on to what has been, and it creates inner turmoil as our outer self no longer matches the environment it's in. When you keep your focus on the path of the soul, you realize that the environment you are in can do very little to influence your well-being. Be willing to redefine yourself by what the new you needs, and let go of the you that's been created. You do this by understanding that the goal in life isn't to take with you everything you've ever done, but instead, meet the person you've become in the process of doing what you've done.

The ephemeral nature of this life means that all we ever actually get to build are sand castles. We might spend ten months or ten years building our particular sand castle but the tides of time will inevitably come up and wash what we've built away. Most people respond by trying to fight back against the tide which yields nothing but frustration as what we've built slowly erodes anyway. You see this when people are clinging to an identity they no longer have. Famous people who try to remain famous turn themselves into a caricature of who they used to be. Relationships that have passed their shelf life and aren't serving our evolution any longer become filled with resentment and stagnation. Instead, we should realize that as long as the kid is still around, we have the opportunity to take what we've learned and build a new sand castle somewhere else. Perhaps with someone else. The tide that's rising is just telling us that it's time. To fight the change in life is to take your shovel and pail and to start scooping water back into the ocean. It will always be futile.

If you are overwhelmed by starting over in life, you are assuredly focusing on the wrong details. Instead, recognize that you still carry the skills you attained in the last build and that just because it's difficult to build a new one doesn't mean it's not worth it. Each time we get to experience something new we learn more about ourselves and the world around us. Change management always comes down to ego management. The thing that makes you a hero in your own story is facing the inevitable death of your thought processes, ideas, and yourself as you know it, and then choosing to answer the call anyway, growing into who the call is asking you to be.

The hero is an adventurer at heart and the adventurer always chooses the path that winds along steep and narrow cliffs over the paved sidewalk because they know if they don't, their soul will pay the price. The safe route and the route that will yield growth are almost always different. The thing about having two paths to choose from is that one will most likely seem easier than the other and that one will probably be at odds with the right one. The person who ignores her own call will continue to feel estranged from herself and the world around her, all the while, the answer to her misery lies on the ignored path. It is not until the discontent of not knowing ourselves outweighs the fear of falling to the jagged rocks below the steep narrow path of the cliff, that we will decide to answer the call.

Ignoring who you really are and what you really want can be comforting for a time as you receive outside validation for your ability to conform but there will be no meaning found in this life. When you begin diving inward and prioritizing the voice within, instead of the many outside voices that surround you, you proactively build resilience. You create a sound frame that the world cannot penetrate because you're no longer asking it for validation. It is only when we truly don't know ourselves that we are susceptible to losing ourselves in our surroundings.

The ability to reinvent yourself by your own volition instead of having the world do it for you is a sign that you're in touch with the adventurer within. The road that leads to such a place of authentic reinvention is one that many never get too. Most of us have a view of ourselves that is so incomplete it could hardly be considered ourselves at all. Your ego has a vested interest in keeping you unaware of all that you really are and you must overcome this interest if you're ever going to grow into who you're meant to be.

To avoid the pitfalls, it always helps to identify them first. There are many roads that will land you with an inauthentic life and while it is your programming that determines much of your decisions, it is the disposition of your personality that will determine the path that you take. There are two main routes that land people with a life that feels light on meaning and connection.

The first is well documented. It resides around doing what you're told you should do. It is the safe path that others, who have a vested interest in your well-being, will encourage you to take. This path is represented by all of the things that you think you should do but deep down don't actually want to do. In many cases it is this outside pressure to live by others desires that compel us to make choices that we wouldn't otherwise make. This path almost always ends at the golden handcuffs. We become so attached to the luxuries that our path provides that we feel as though we can't live without them.

Although the pressure to be a certain thing in the eyes of the world does exist, we give that pressure far more dominion over us with our own internal expectations. Many times, we make a decision to take a path that feels wrong for us because we've allowed our own psyche to put walls around us that were never there. In many cases, people do have an idea about what they want you to be, but we give that idea far too much emphasis within our own minds. The process of knowing what you really want is the process of deconstructing these walls.

As the walls come down, what you find is that no one was ever actually that concerned with what you do or don't do in the first place. Most people are stuck inside their own walls and they are far too deep in their own insecurities to see what anyone else might be up to, let alone actually care beyond a short remark to prop up their own sense of self. Note that this isn't always the case, because many times our parents or superiors do have high expectations for what we should be. If you carry those expectations into adulthood, you really need to rethink the amount of power you give other people over your life. The job of a parent, for example, is to raise you. Once that is done, we must transition our relationship from one of authority to one of council. If we don't, we will be forever trapped in the need for approval.

The second path to a life you don't recognize as authentic is found in the complete opposite direction. It is the path of the rebel. It is a systemic need to shed others standards for your life and if left unchecked it becomes just as dangerous to authenticity as conformity. The rebel's choices arise out of a deep desire to prove their independence to the world. If they aren't aware, the rebel may end up prioritizing being different, even when it's not advantageous.

The path of living by one's own truth can be intoxicating to the rebel and this intoxication is even furthered by the on-lookers admiration. We are inherently drawn to people that blaze their own trail, possibly because it comes innate with a hope for a better tomorrow. If nothing else, they often inspire us to lean into the parts of ourselves that long for a new world. The person with a natural inclination toward conformity may be mystified by the rebel's ability to live with such freedom that he seems to make his own choices and live by his own rules and on some level long for such freedom within his own life. This admiration in turn often emboldens the rebel's resolve to stay on his own path, but looks can be deceiving. The rebel could be a slave to his own ideals just as the conformist could be a slave to the world. We're all fighting our own battles and carrying our own cross.

It's important to remember that your natural inclinations are just that. Natural inclinations. They aren't a hint toward a superior mode of being in the world and the person that believes they are, likely lives in delusion. The balanced equation of the universe is set to ensure that we all have our own cross to bear. We all have parts of our own humanity that we must seek to overcome so that we can show up in the world in a way that feels right for us. We are all struggling through this human experience in our own way. It's easy to look at people that are having success in a certain area of life and make assumptions about the rest of their lives. Often the view we get is of the outside and the assumptions we make are about the inside. The truth is that beautiful and successful people that we admire take their own lives every day. At the same time, people with very little material wealth find themselves abundantly happy all of the time. Outer success and inner peace aren't necessarily correlated. It is only humans who appear to be hell bent on acting as if they are.

We are always choosing between one of two paths in every aspect of our lives. If we want peace in this chaotic world, then we have to show up for ourselves when it counts and be brave enough to choose the right path, even when an easier one inevitably exists. When we don't feel like we have multiple options to choose from in life, it is because we are too embedded in it to recognize that other options exist.

If your view is too myopic to your own problems, you will never be able to frame them in a way that gives you the space to make a different decision. Fish can't see the water and we can't see the air. It is entirely possible that you might be a slave to your idea of what consists of a good life and feel forced into decisions that are in accordance with that life. It's also just as likely that you are driven by a rejection of that life. In either case, you won't see the option to live differently from how you have always existed if you are a slave to your own ideals. People that are rebellious by nature get so caught up in proving that they don't need the status quo that they are unable to see some of the benefits of what the status quo might be able to offer.

This might also be seen in the life of the person who dedicates his life to an altruistic path. These types of people get so caught up in their beliefs about what is "right" that they have trouble seeing things like money as any value to their lives. As such, they are less effective at carrying out their true desires for good in the first place. Many of us end up knowing deep down that we want and need a more authentic life, but we simply can't let go of our ideals long enough to get what we want. It might be that what you can't let go of is the representation of your steep and narrow path on the cliffs.

To find our unique path, we must meditate on and ask ourselves, who we are beyond who and what the world expects us to be. Find this answer and the world will have far less success in bending you to its will. We are conditioned to rely on authority, elders, and existing power structures in order to give us the answers that we need. Many of us go our entire lives looking for solutions out in the world to problems that are happening within us. Unfortunately, what we tend to find in all of our searching is only distraction. The world is not short on shiny objects that will keep you busy while the dreams you have are inviting you to find yourself in their pursuit.

Eventually, you will find that there is only one path that has the answers you need. Unfortunately, you are the only one who knows what it is. You look at the world in a way that is uniquely you and as such, your path is based on your subjectivity. There are struggles that were meant for your solutions, lessons that hold the next steps toward your higher self and potential that can only be unlocked by the key you have. You are the adventurer and so the adventure can only be your own.

Chapter 11

WHAT IF IT'S NOT THE WORST THING THAT HAS EVER HAPPENED TO YOU?

"When written in Chinese, the word "crisis" is composed of two characters - one represents danger and the other represents opportunity."

— John F Kennedy

One of the most difficult parts of life is accepting that your invitation to live deeper and to be more could feel like the absolute worst thing that has ever happened to you. Many of us go through these difficulties all the time but we frame them in a way that isn't necessarily helpful and because of this they don't feel like an invitation at all. Our pain often becomes something we must simply get through or survive. We shouldn't forget that many people's lives are made much better because someone else went through something painful and refused to let others live with that same fate. There isn't a thing that you enjoy in this life which someone before you hadn't previously suffered for. That is how the world evolves and continues to improve. All you have to do is play your part and pay it forward. It happens to be the least and most you could possible do with your life.

There is an invitation to make the world (consequently, your world) a better place buried in every difficult thing that you go through. You have an ability to harbor two extremely different mindsets when dealing with adversity and while both are available to you, the one that you choose to adopt will make all of the difference in the world when it comes to your long term success and finding the right path for you.

Often due to a lack of perspective, we have a propensity to get caught up in the negative minutiae of what we endure. We unknowingly prioritize things that don't really matter in the broad sense of our lives, while allowing our neurosis to dictate our emotional state. When we go through something (such as loss) we have a tendency to obsess over things we can't change and we become angry in the wake of a reality that doesn't match the one that we had envisioned or hoped for ourselves. This affinity to dwell on our difficulties is the default human reaction due to the fact that we have evolved to be particularly sensitive to negative situations. This is especially seen when we aren't the ones who make the decision that lands us in turmoil, but rather are thrust into a new circumstance for which we aren't ready. This can happen when we are fired, or broken up with, or find ourselves at the behest of malevolence. We replay what went wrong over and over, hoping that enough reminiscence will bring us an understanding that eases our pain. Only it never does.

Our world is structured in such a way that we are always only one move or conversation away from chaos. One diagnosis, one break up, one loss of a job, one wrongdoing, or one false step can sling us into complete catastrophe and it can happen in a single moment. You are either going through something hard now, or you will be in the future. When you are, things that have always made sense suddenly never made sense. People you have always known suddenly feel like strangers. The cosmos, God, gods, or whatever you believe in, which once seemed to be just and operating out of a sense of order, will begin to appear cruel and vindictive upon further inspection. This can quickly conjure feelings of anxiety, anger, sadness, embarrassment, shame, or even an amalgamation of them all. Interestingly, many people would be surprised to know that the half-life of those emotions is actually quite short. While it changes from person to person, anger for example, typically only lasts long enough for your sympathetic nervous system to return to its original state. Yet, how many of us choose to hold on to anger long after our physiological response of an increased heart rate and hypertension has subsided? We don't let it go for days or even weeks. If we never feel that the original grievance is rectified, it's possible that we will hold on to that anger long enough to let it become us. We will walk around perpetually angry every day. Eventually, if it goes unchecked, that will become the fabric from which our lives are made. Anger has a way of anchoring our hearts and not allowing any other emotions to exist in that space. We say that we have anger problems but it is more appropriate to say that the anger has us.

To make matters worse, anger is also a costly emotion as it tends to use up biological resources faster than any other emotions. In fact, it is the one emotion that we can prove which has the ability to manifest itself physically. The anger that you feel compelled to hold on to is unequivocally linked to early death by heart disease and stroke.

There is however, a second mode of being in the world. It requires you to live and to let go. Not because the other person or the situation deserves it (they probably don't), but because you do. Resentment will breed contempt, and contempt will turn your life into a living hell. You don't deserve to live in hell any longer. Plain and simple. To get to the second mode of being, start by asking yourself a simple question. "Why is this happening for me, instead of to me?" If you think earnestly, you will eventually come up with a reason, and that reason matters because it will help you shift your thought process about what comes next. This isn't a call for positive self-talk that doesn't match the reality in which you are living. This isn't easy. This is looking chaos directly in the face and asking it for answers -- even if those answers aren't going to pleasant to face. Understanding that everything is happening for you isn't about trying to change reality, it's about choosing to face struggle in a productive manner.

You have to look hard to find the beneficial side of pain but there is always one that exists. If you are able to pinpoint it, you can begin to start rebuilding your life on that reason. You can take a step forward in the middle of high winds. Regardless of how small that step might be, forward progress should never be discounted. The significance of this mental shift is the determinant between whether this thing you are going through will be a catalyst for expansion or diminishment. Will you get closer to or further away from the person you were meant to be as a result of what you're going through? That's a choice that only you get to make and it's only you that will have to live with the consequences of whatever you choose. Many people look at what's negative and then complain about not being happy. As a general rule you are going to go where you're focus is. Are you focused on solutions or problems? That will determine where you end up. Furthermore, greatness in your life isn't dictated by your present situation or your past circumstances. The only person that inevitably allows your "right now" difficulties to become your forever situation is you. You have to be sure that you don't let the negative emotion of a difficult situation anchor your heart or there simply won't be room for anything else. Humans have the uncanny ability to turn an hour long physiological response into a mode of being and it kills our forward progress.

As you reflect on tragic moments in your own life, perhaps in the past or presently, you have to ask yourself productive questions that help you reframe the way you are thinking about what you are going through. What if this wasn't the worst thing to happen to you? What if you began to find reasons why it's even good, or at least tolerable for the time being? What if finding the reason that things are happening for you instead of to you is the foundation from which you get to build a life that is bigger and better than even the reality that you had first envisioned for yourself? The fact that life has the ability to be greater than we ever imagined is reason enough not to hold on too tightly to what we imagined. This is actually the beauty in realizing the simplicity of our minds in comparison to the cosmos. They have more in store for you than you have the capacity to even realize, should you decide to let go and accept the invitation. It can take long periods of time screwing things up and forcing things, only to have them not work out, for you to begin understanding that you don't necessarily know what's best.

While you can't do anything about the initial response of your nervous system, you can do much about the way you choose to view your subsequent days. There is no question that life is full of struggle and pain that we are ill equipped to handle. This isn't an excuse to blow past emotions and not feel them. In many cases, feeling is the only way through. Since the nature of our reality is such that one conversation can change the entire trajectory of our lives, to not feel hurt, sad, lonely, or angry in the wake of pain would be to deny reality, which isn't a great basis for changing it. It is also often the very fact that we feel those negative emotions in the first place that inspire us to change the world for the better. Remember, we don't get to choose our catalysts for potential. We can only respond with as much light as possible.

To take that a step further, when you decide to be a light amidst the dark because of something that happened to you, you not only light the way for others, but for yourself. It is often your ability to help others which leads you to a fuller expression of yourself. It is why it is happening for you and not to you. That doesn't mean you allow it to be justifiable. We should always take arms up against injustice. It just means we aren't simply accepting and being victimized by the events that take place during the course of our lives. We are pushing back against it, and consequently becoming more of who we should be in the process. The problem is, when you choose to let a negative emotion weave itself into who you are, you have no room or emotional capacity left to embrace the beauty in your life that still exists. Don't excuse it, just forgive it. Make room in your heart and your life for what is to come. We are wired to prevail against the storm but that is only possible if we don't succumb to it.

Although it doesn't seem fair, in many cases, the complete upheaval of our lives is our call to adventure. It is our chance to burn the old and create the new. Our initial default mode forces us to want to protect what we have as if it is all that we will ever have, but anyone who has been through hard times in the past knows that it always gets better. The human spirit is resilient beyond measure. With enough fortitude, we are always sure to see the sun rise again, regardless of the storms that surround us. Sometimes, we protect things and hold onto them longer than we should and the universe comes along and pries them from us. This is especially true with relationships and jobs that don't serve our long term growth. It hurts, it sucks, and it isn't fair. Life isn't easy but it is worth it. The happiness found in operating out of a life of meaning far outweighs the storms that we have to pass through in order to get there. The stories in history that we remember happen because a greater life existed on the right side of a great collapse, not the left. The catch is, you have to open yourself up to viewing your new situation as an opportunity for what is to come. You are in the middle of a death sentence but it's not meant for you, only the life that wasn't going to serve you in the long run anyway. Don't adopt it as your own because you aren't willing to let go of what can never, and will never, be changed. Try to look at the landscape for what it has the opportunity to be and not what it currently is.

What dream or desire have you held onto that you might be free to now pursue? You will always find one if you ask yourself honestly. You might have to get quiet to hear the answer because after a while of being ignored, the universe will stop asking. Now, in the midst of whatever you are going through, might be a good time to begin asking yourself what you really want or what you really feel drawn to. You may just find that now you are free to finally pursue it. It is often rock bottom that serves as the foundation for the most incredible structures that we know today.

Regardless of how small our lives might seem in the moment; we each have our own spot in the unfolding of the universe. In this regard, our lives have importance beyond our comprehension. You and your time here are no more important than that of early man and no less important than that of the greatest world leaders. The large size of a machine doesn't imply that you can discount the importance of any of its parts. They are all needed. Size and value aren't related in that way. Humans have an affinity to get wrapped up in the negative and small. Our second mindset, the one that is available to everyone simply because we have our own spot in this great cosmic unfolding, is to reach for the awe inspiring. Great people aren't born that way, they simply answer their invitations, trusting that the cosmos will sort out the details. It is important to recognize that those details might not be sorted out in the timeline that you want. You can't compare how quickly one person might obtain results to your particular path. The chance that you might need this particular setback in order to prevail for the future in store for you is just too great to be calculated. There are simply too many factors to be considered and we don't have all the details. You have to trust the process, not the timeline.

When you are in the middle of heartache or catastrophe, the term "everything happens for a reason" can feel more like a pejorative critique of your inability to overcome than heartfelt condolences. This phrase only becomes profound when you begin to understand that everything happens for a reason AND that you have the opportunity to find that reason. The fact that you can assign a justification to your pain shouldn't be overlooked as it literally puts the power back in your hands. It gives you something to grasp and helps you begin to restore order in the middle of chaos. The situation at hand may be out of your hands, but what comes next is squarely in your control.

To be completely honest with you, I struggled putting this chapter in the book. I understand all too well how the personal development industry can be coated in unhelpful drivel perpetuated by people that haven't dealt with life's deeper issues, only to prey on the people that have. But this goes hand in hand with one of the theories posited in this book, which is that everything we do matters. Finding a reason in your struggle is the difference between not only building your life into all that it could be, but also in helping untold amounts of others build theirs as well You never know what the hand you lend to someone else might mean.

We all know that when a child is learning to walk, the option to give up after they fall really doesn't exist. If a child were to decide to stay down after a tumble, the rest of his life would undoubtedly become a failure. What we fail to realize is that if we also fail to get back up after a fall, our lives will become failures as well. The good news is that regardless of the pain and the struggle involved, as long as you have another breath, the ability to get back up is always a choice that you have.

The fact that the world we live has built in mechanisms to teach you what you need to know in order to move to considerably higher levels in life is nothing short of astounding. For us, the ones who often find ourselves feeling victimized by this same mechanism, it is important that we come up with a way in which we can think about and ultimately shoulder whatever it is that threatens to tear us apart. Similar to finding a productive worldview, we must conceptualize our pain in a way that positions us to deal with it appropriately. In my first book *Burn Your Couch*, I delved into physical pain quite extensively as I've often found physical endeavors have a way of breathing life into us. As our hopes for what we could be clash against our perceived physical limitations, our character and fortitude find their footing in that fight. For the purposes of this book, I'd like to keep the philosophy centered around emotional pain. It is far less tangible and it is often the catalyst for a new narrative in your head. When we don't approach emotional pain correctly, it has a way of walling us into a smaller mode of being. We become closed off to more possibilities as we recognize that some of those possibilities will inevitably hold more pain. We become the ones who look our dragon in the eye and choose not to engage.

I find our framing of emotional pain to be fascinating in that it's here to teach us lessons and hand us information that we clearly need, yet we will spend our entire lives taking different roads home just so that we don't ever have to confront what hurt us. When we are in pain, we think back on better times and long for our lives to hold them again. We self soothe with a host of different resources. Yet, in the end, not one of those self-soothing methods will lend themselves to transcendence. Pain is a blinding feeling. When it is acute enough, there is nothing else to feel. When we find ourselves square in the center of pain, it is as if we are in a car that is overheating. The alarms are yelling at us, the gauges are all pegged and tell us nothing, and what we really need is to pull over and let the damn thing cool off. Instead, we tend to keep our foot on the gas and turn to something that causes a dopamine response to provide temporary relief and anesthetic. What we fail to realize is that retail therapy isn't actually therapy. It is a band-aid at best. You don't need more things, you need to turn the engine off for a minute so that you can diagnose what you have there. You need to realize that although it hurts, there is something that you need to know. In that way, pain is the best teacher that we have. If you think about the biggest moments of transformation in your life, you will almost assuredly realize that those moments came on the back of something painful.

What it means to be human is that we live through seasons that encompass the entire spectrum of the human condition. Pain always finds itself in that spectrum because when times are good, we tend to become closed off to learning, and evolution becomes slowed. When pain gives you the feedback that something is amiss, we find ourselves open to the possibility of what that thing could be, so that we can transcend that season in our lives. What we often perceived as wrong is typically a catalyst for evolution. To live with your eyes open and to continue moving forward regardless is the most courageous position that a human can take. When you live long enough, you become privy to the burden of being. You will catch glimpses of yourself where you caused pain to other people, and likewise when those people caused pain for you. Comparing that pain with the vast space that surrounds us can begin to make us feel like the entire thing is frivolous and cruel. This inevitably causes feelings of guilt and shame which of course does nothing for the full expression of who we are. Those feelings only serve to keep us there and add unnecessary suffering to our pain.

You will suffer to the extent that you are resisting what hurts. Our pain is manifested in different situations and forms throughout our lives but if you can get to the core of it, what you realize is that deep down this repeating scenario is happening because of a scar that you've never allowed yourself to address. If for nothing else, this is reason enough to let yourself be whatever it is that you are actually feeling. Even if that feeling is hurt. Sit with it and be where you're at so that once and for all you can heal from what's hurt you. It may be necessary to seek professional help from someone who has learned the ability to sift through your layers and get to the heart of the problem. Whatever the cost of that is, to your ego or to your pocketbook, you have got to face it so that you don't live in your own drama for seventy years and then call it a life. This is the inherent problem of the self-soothing methods that we use to get out of our painful times. Instead, leave space for how and what you feel, and understand that it is the acceptance of your pain that will mark the end of your suffering.

Chapter 12

SAGE ADVICE FOR THE DRIVEN

"Details of your incompetence do not interest me."
— Miranda Priestly, from the film,
The Devil Wears Prada

For those of us that seek to be high achievers, ambition has a tendency to become the inadvertent God we serve. We treat ambition itself as if it will yield results worth attaining as long as we have enough of it. It is a lot like money in that it will help get you where you want to go, but it has very little to offer when it becomes the place that you go. Very little at the end of any road paved with material success will actually satiate for any period of time. Rampant ambition is yet another symptom of a culture that underserves the soul.

Typically, there are only a few destinations that a life of unadulterated ambition will lead you. After the ego (which uses ambition as its chief method of moving through the world) has finally had its fill and you still aren't satisfied, what you find is that your soul is left to clean up the mess and lead you out of it. Often, this requires a great humility, the active reconciliation of things that have gone amiss, and perhaps two or three more ego deaths along the way. If you haven't allowed your ego to drive your life into a complete mess, you will most likely end up looking around your garage wondering what else life might hold for you. In this case, the soul is left to keep the kingdom afloat that has been built by the ego. The soul may or may not care about what you built when you felt like you weren't good enough without building something. It is often in these moments when you see an existential crisis arise. This is when we realize that the ladders we've spent our life climbing don't lead to the promised end state. Only more rungs and more climbing.

At its worst, when ambition is allowed to run without restraint, it is a chaotic drive on a bumpy road that leads to no place in particular besides more roads and more bumps. When you are always traveling and never pulling over, it can be tough to enjoy the scenery. People end up hurt and things get broken as the unguided ambitious person often leaves a wake of carnage in his path. Mindfulness doesn't have to run counter to drive, but it often does, as the ambitious person tends to have lots of things to do but not enough time to do them. The checklist becomes the manifesto, and the achievement becomes the symbol of happiness. The list provides the feeling of forward progress which temporarily quells the soul. Unfortunately, real happiness is often traded for momentary pleasure. Material can't buy you happiness, but it does have a monopoly on the pleasure game. What the flesh wants, the flesh can buy. Humans are extremely susceptible to being blinded by ambition, allowing our passion to override our discernment. We want what we want, and when we put what we want above everything else, our ambition will see that we get it. It is here that we begin the process of learning through pain. When we finally reconcile our actions and the people we hurt in order to get what the ego desires, we can finally start to push on in a meaningful direction and choose to learn through love.

This is all part of the process of what it means to be human. It's easy to beat yourself up for mistakes you made when you didn't know better but it helps to understand that in reality, you were forced to navigate the world as an ill-equipped and scared little kid. You may still be. We mess things up. We self-sabotage. We convince ourselves whole heartedly that we want what we say we want, and we make terrible decisions along the way to get it. We don't go through these things because we were put on Earth to be perfect. We go through these things because the human that we become on the other side of them is worth every second of it. To free yourself of the places your ambition has brought you, you must only understand that you don't actually need them. If I were to tell you to push harder to be someone else and try more things in order to get somewhere, it might make you comfortable and back up your world view, and it might trend on social media, but it won't get you contentment. That's going to be found on the path you are yet to take.

A new way of being requires a new way of viewing. This is when you begin to understand that you don't actually need anything outside of yourself, which is a super power in the era of "keeping up with the Joneses." When you don't need something in your life is when you can actually use it to improve your life. When you think you need something, you add a hint of desperation to your action. Desperate people tend to do stupid things in the name of what they want. Maybe you can relate? I know that I can. At its best, when the proper aim is found, ambition will lead you home. Every task, goal, and achievement you succeed in will bring you closer to the person that you were meant to be. Every failure will serve the same purpose, pointing out errors in your current operating system. This is only possible when you understand that you already have what you need in order to thrive in this life thus making you free to line up your ambition with your values.

Another side effect of unchecked ambition is that when it shows you a wrong turn or something that must be improved upon, you are likely to think it's just another thing in your way to be pushed over or driven through. As far as tools go, ambition is a hammer. If you apply it to every job that comes along, there will be some destruction that takes place. You will get everything to fit, but at what cost? When ambition becomes the "thing" in your life instead of the mechanism that helps you get to the thing, your decisions gradually become more robotic as you prioritize forward progress over everything else. You have no doubt seen this archetype before. It is often seen in the business person that prioritizes profit over people. It is dramatized in *A Christmas Carol* by Charles Dickens with the character, Ebenezer Scrooge. This was made popular because humans who read it recognized the deep truth hidden in the fiction. It is all too easy to lose track of what is real and what matters when you are looking through the lens of unbridled ambition for material gain. The problem with becoming robotic in your actions as you move through life is that at the end of the day, you still have to contend with being human and you still have to exist in the world with other humans. When drive is your motivator, the chances of you alienating those other humans becomes significantly greater. Regardless of how much you pacify yourself with more drive, more tasks, and more achievements, there is a void you won't be able to fill with any amount of to-do lists.

We all have basic human needs, and a connection to the people that we are sharing this experience with is one of those needs. Regardless of your independence, that need has some role within your life. There is no getting around it. The question you have to ask yourself is, "Am I willing to let the ambition in my life exist in place of contentment?" For a lot of people, the answer is yes, only because they haven't gotten far enough down the road of being discontent to know how painful it actually gets.

People often find that as they begin to grow their ambition, it is hard to exist on that level for long. In light of this, they craft a sort of persona to help breathe life into their efforts and alienate them from the people that would slow them down. The most recent way this archetype has played itself out in our culture is in the "boss babe": archetype. The shadow of this is seen in the movie, *The Devil Wears Prada*, where ambition becomes all that matters. Please hear me correctly on this; It's not that to strive as a woman is a problem, it's that to strive as anyone from a place of inauthenticity is going to rob you of a complete life. You have to know when to put the persona on and when to take it off. When your persona becomes your only gear, what you find is that you can't connect with people. That is because it is a coping mechanism – it is not the real you.

Consider the relationships you have in this life and the ones you really prize. Most likely, the ones you hold the closest are the ones where you can enter into a space and just be truly you. This is because, again, you can't connect with someone from your coping mechanisms, even if the way that you cope is prized by the society in which you live. Ambition is a coping mechanism for many in western culture. The body of work in my own life shifted dramatically with this very realization. As a student of human potential, I found myself focused heavily on the physiology of high achievement, specifically that which is associated with endurance sports. For me, every finish line became the start of the search for the next. While there is something to be said for this mentality, and the results it can breed, contentment won't be one of those results. Every accomplishment brought me a little more emptiness as I put my hope for a better life in the next achievement. Trust me when I say that if you find yourself alone and frustrated for answers, it won't matter what you accomplish along the way.

Unfortunately, most people don't consider the implications of their misguided drive. Instead they simply accept the void as a necessary byproduct of life on the go. They feel as if drive and peace do not have the ability to coexist. If you are driven and have lost all semblance of peace in your life, or if you find that you have less connection with the people and the world around you, then it is time to come to grips with the fact that your drive needs to be realigned.

Beyond the isolation that unchecked ambition has the ability to create, you also run the risk of losing yourself completely to your ambition. It is possible to keep some connections in your life, but have no idea who you are outside of your chosen endeavor. Your identity will become so wrapped up in what you are doing, that the "you" which existed prior to the task or endeavor will cease to exist completely. Your essence can be hijacked and temporarily lost to your drive. If this is you, take solace in the fact that the light within is never truly extinguished.

I wonder how many high performers would crumble into an existentially depressed mess if you were to take away their ability to perform in their chosen arena? I wonder if you might be the same way? When people fail to understand that they are so much more than what they do, it is only a matter of time before they find themselves in chaos, grasping at an identity that no longer exists. When you give your identity away to your ambitions, you are building your psyche on a house of cards. Even if your chosen endeavor makes you seem mentally tough, you are, in fact, fragile to an unsettling degree. This is seen in the NFL player that loses his career to injury before it ever really gets going. Not losing yourself to your pursuits is one of the most difficult things a driven person will ever face. Keep yourself in the game by understanding that it is just that, a game. One of the many that you will play while you are here.

This further illustrates the point for having an overall aim that is rooted in values and not things or achievements. A proper aim in the world is akin to an athletic stance in sports. A slight bend in the knee while having your feet wide enough apart will make you resilient to being shoved over. When your ambitions control the trajectory of your aim, your feet are together and your knees are locked out. It won't be difficult for something to come along and shove you down, regardless of how strong you are. Life is hard enough without leaving yourself completely vulnerable to the tough times of circumstance. You are better off putting ambition in the passenger seat so you call the shots and fortify your mentality. If you don't, you are giving the keys to your psyche up to an unreliable drunk, and hoping he can drive you home. You will endure great emotional highs and lows as you subject yourself to the behest of all that could go wrong and all that could go right. As anyone who has ever done anything great in life can tell you, there is much more of the former. When you lose yourself to your ambition, unforeseen obstacles no longer become only about finding a way forward, but also about finding yourself as every threat to the task becomes a personal threat to who you are.

In this case, catastrophe has the ability to derail you completely. Why would you want to leave your emotional health and happiness up to the whims of everyday things that go wrong? Markets turn downward all the time. Athletes blow out their ACLs all the time. People get fired all the time. People disappoint each other all the time. Are you willing to keep standing in the gauntlet with your legs locked out and your feet together?

In order to avoid this, you must realize that your value as a human being comes from the soul that sits behind the human. The characteristics of the soul will get you exactly where you want to be. Those characteristics include unconditional love, compassion, understanding, your ability to take care of yourself and others, your ability to grow, evolve and learn, and inspire others to do the same. Stake your life's mission on the intangibles and use the tangibles to further that mission. That way, if the metrics are ever taken away from you or put into question, they don't have the ability to take the mission away completely. What you find when you are rooted in the correct mission and you are living up to your own internal value system, is that the human being has the incredible capacity to hold multiple feelings and emotions at once. Life can be hard, but you can still appreciate the beauty that surrounds you. Times can be tough, and you can still be grateful for the opportunities that you have. Don't let ambition take up all of your bandwidth when you have the capacity for so much more.

Regardless of the pressure that the world puts on you to produce the metrics, you can't compromise who you are for the process. The minute you do, you become unfit for service because your mental health is on borrowed time and mentally unhealthy people can't serve at their full capacity until they work through what ails them. That is the case regardless of how much they accomplish while using ambition to cover up those ailments. If there is anything the world needs, it is your service. You are more useful to yourself and to the world at large when you begin to understand that you are who you are and not what you do.

Now is a good time to start digging deeper into your drives and motivations so that you can ensure that you stay away from the unhelpful lines of thinking and frivolous pursuits in which many people spend their days entrenched. Most people believe that their ambition must be applied within the confines of the constructed world, i.e., you are smart, so you choose a life found in trades that other smart people do. You learn with your hands, so you look for jobs that people tend to do with their dexterity. This is fine if you are happy. But if you aren't, the question is, "Why are you staying in a lane that doesn't serve you?" Your ambition can be applied to creating a new world for yourself altogether, if that is what you choose. The social world has been constructed, which means you can take it apart and construct it in any way that you like. That requires you to get outside of the perspective that's making you think you can't. More ambition won't serve you in lieu of a creative angle.

The World Health Organization reports that the current average life expectancy is sixty-nine point eight years for males and seventy four point two years for females. Because I know you can read, you have already burned through some of that time. With whatever you have left, it is not reasonable to think that you should spend even a second of that time holding yourself back from the life that you deserve because you don't want to believe that you are good enough for whatever you want. It's also not reasonable to assume that you should eat up that time with ego driven pursuits of ambition without the proper thought behind them. This is why you have to take the time to do the deep emotional work to heal yourself from your past. Otherwise, you will relive it over and over, and end up calling it a life. Ambition will mean a lot more when it's applied in a direction that's actually right for you. Most of us are keeping our foot on the gas without realizing we are still in the roundabout. Humans are inherently goal oriented and adaptable creatures. The main way that we judge the success of our own lives is by how well we measure up to our own goals. We push off into the unknown in order to conquer what we might, knowing that the road along the way will hold more for our lives than the routine and predictable ever could. We understand that in daring greatly enough to push down the road that holds all possible outcomes for our future, we are simultaneously expanding our consciousness and learning more about what it really means to be alive.

Technically speaking, a goal should be something that pulls you toward it, while a motivator should be something that pushes you forward toward whatever that thing is. Due to the fact that most people don't know themselves very well at all, they set goals that once achieved have pulled them outside of their own value system. To further complicate matters, they remain oblivious to what it is that is actually driving them forward. Another problem arises for people when they find their motivators are at odds with their goals. You know what you want, but the things that are subconsciously pushing you along are pushing you in a different direction from what you explicitly want. This could be the case if you want to start a new business but your internal drive for safety will see that you self-sabotage your own success in order to keep you at your safe job with your safe paycheck. People often try to just do more, or try harder when they fail, but it's worth noting that ambition isn't an adequate replacement for learning from failure. As is the case with most people, you will find yourself somewhere in the middle of competing ideologies, completely frustrated as the results you want are inconsistent with the results that you get. The space between the cautious mind and the daring heart can be an emotionally brutal way to spend your time as indecision and dreams left with loose ends stay in the back of your mind like an app that you never closed out of your phone. Because most of us are driven by survival, we tend to make small minded decisions as we worship at the altar of safety and comfort. We internally reason that if we aim small, we will miss small and can easily survive any negative experiences that result. But we aren't here to play small. Life in and of itself is such an extraordinarily sublime organization of energy, that to allow that energy to vibrate at a low frequency is to miss the full joy that it holds for us. We have to correct our internal drives and keep them in the proper perspective so that as the universe calls us to a more daring life, we have what it takes to actually answer that call.

There are many times when our calling in life will have us take off the bow line and set sail without being able to visualize the destination. It is here that the human finds their true metal. When working toward a known safe end, we are often sailing but never too far from the shore. It is when you battle the elements and lose track of the safe shore that your character is forged.

For many high achievers, ambition is the thing that makes them feel safe. You don't ever have to grapple with the existential nature of being if you just keep yourself entrenched in doing. Forward progress soothes the psyche... at least until we realize we don't know what we are moving toward. While a lack of ambition can certainly create the condition for a stagnant life, it is the overly ambitious that tend to drive too far from the correct path. What we must remember is that ambition is an engine, but it is not a destination. It is a strong desire to do or achieve something, typically requiring determination and hard work. It carries with it no inherent purpose, goal, or objective outside of forward progress. The proper role of ambition is one that sees it removed from the driver's seat in your life. It shouldn't call the shots, only help you apply your foot to the gas pedal. When ambition becomes its own self-serving motivator, you are likely to wind up in a place that you don't recognize very well at all. Any chimp can hustle harder for the sake of it, but an evolved human has the option of using cognition to discern when to drive, when to hit the brakes, and when the roads aren't worth traveling.

Chapter 13

LOVE, MONEY, AND CULTURE

"Love in its essence is spiritual fire."

— Senneca

Due to the fact that our environment plays such a big role in how we show up in this life, it is only logical that we should explore the culture that we're born into and how that might be affecting our experience. Culture serves as another level of analysis to identify how the human evolves. Further, if it is through knowing ourselves that we are able to actually affect change with authority in our lives, then it is through knowing our culture that we are able to start making changes for many people's lives.

This is often the most difficult layer of our lives to pull apart because we are embedded in our culture. This is similar to the way that it is difficult to know whether or not we are dreaming while asleep at night. Where does experience end and dream begin? Where does culture end and where do you begin? These things can be hard to parse out. Where it can be difficult to identify things that are contributing to a whole is when those things become so integrated into the whole that we fail to recognize the ways that they are individually directing our lives. If you can isolate a particular symptom, you stand a better chance at identifying an ailment. Said another way, you can often look at an end state and reverse engineer the problem to figure out how an end state came to be. This to be the most useful way of dissecting a culture.

First, we need a little bit of context. The world has been here for a very long time. We have not. Due to the fact that you've been here for such a short time, it can be easy to fall into the line of thinking that what you've been given has always been and always will be, and that there are parts of our lives that are immovable or beyond questioning. If I could change one thing about the way that we see the world collectively, it would be to say that nothing is beyond questioning. The way that you see the world is a product of the world that you have experienced. Many of your thoughts and values serve as a timestamp based on the culture that you were born into.

Many of us are wired to accept given processes that we have been indoctrinated into (such as that of a lifestyle that includes a nine-to-five job and a value set that pushes off happiness until Friday night) and that lack of questioning about the structure of our lives leaves us with few options when they turn out to be less than we had hoped. If something can be questioned, you are at least opening up the possibility of change. Changing ourselves requires deep objective introspection. Changing culture requires that, plus an ability to analyze processes at a macro level and the courage to question them. The reason that courage is so heavily required to make changes within our lives is because in many ways, our culture is a tyrant. It dictates what is acceptable, what is punishable and what is considered good order. It funnels you into a way of thinking, and it chastises you with the collective when you wander too far from that way of thinking. After having a certain way of thinking pushed on you for multiple decades, especially while you are forming the substructure of your world through your beliefs, it can be difficult to realize that as an adult, the pressure you feel into that way of thinking is implied but it's no longer mandated.

For most of the history of our culture, the only way to really get outside of that way of thinking was to be disruptive in a way that delivered people something so positive or so desired that they were willing to overlook your disobedience. When you disrupt an industry and give people something that they want or something that makes their lives easier, you are applauded. Such is the case with Steve Jobs or Jeff Bezos, (the founders of Apple inc and Amazon respectively). The problem is that there are only two of them. Everyone else that doesn't fit into the system but can't seem to create a new system altogether, has ended up as an outcast. Our culture punishes divergent ways of thinking by holding necessities of life ransom, such as shelter, food, and water. You either overcome with spectacular results that allow you to provide for yourself or you live on the brink of starvation. If you subjugate yourself enough to work within the confines of a conventional job, then you only starve socially. It's hard to say what is worse.

When you ditch college, forgo the family, and risk it all for a dream that no one can see but you, and that dream fails, the tyrannical culture you live in will give you few options or sympathy. Simply return to the collective and your wounds will heal. You will have to accept a little decay on your soul when the cubicle doesn't allow as much room to roam as you'd like, but at least you will be able to feed yourself and you won't look too dumb with your outlandish dreams or wild speculations on how things might be different.

Conversely, you can continue on your path and risk being so misunderstood that you turn to drugs, sex, and other pacifiers, not as a life enhancements, but as a method of survival. Our culture further chastises these things but what we often fail to recognize is that they are often the only things keeping an outcasted population alive. The psychological pressure that comes innate with the inability to conform is more damaging than most people inside of a system stop to realize. The tyrannical father that is society chastises you for not fitting in, then chastises for how you cope with not fitting in without ever stopping to try to understand that there are humans in the system that aren't biologically wired for the system.

Now however, we are in an interesting time in history where things are starting to change and we should take a moment to reflect on just how lucky we are that that is the case. For a quick lesson in history, there was an asteroid that traveled for billions of years across many galaxies. It traveled so long that our little brains can't even conceptualize that span of time. It then hit an earth that was spinning and it happened to hit a sulfur mine that caused the Ice Age. If it would have hit anywhere else on Earth, life wouldn't have been possible. This stardust happened to find the right elements of water and energy (via lightning storms) to give birth to a single cell organism. That organism would eventually make the leap to us over the course of billions more years of brutally hard fought evolution. I don't care if you believe in divine intervention or the most improbable chances being met of all time. Either way, we are a collection of stardust and chaos and we get to exist when the internet is a thing. And now, you are an adult. The pressure you feel to be something else other than who you really are is unfortunate, but it's not the final say anymore. You can set up your lifestyle in any way that you want, and you can be anything that your mind has the possibility of conceiving. You just have to learn that not only is this all true, but you don't have to apologize for doing this life thing exactly as you want. (Also, how absurd is it that anyone could be the result of massive cosmic collision and then have the audacity to tell someone else that they are doing it wrong? That is honestly so bizarrely comical that it's difficult to describe.)

Even still, our culture continues to dictate our behavior in ways that we might not choose, all things being equal. You have to be hyper aware of how the world is unfolding so that it doesn't funnel you into a lesser way of being. For the evolution of good to prevail, we must continue to question this unfolding, especially if that unfolding is happening in a way that isn't serving everyone. Imagine if no one questioned the way things were shaping up in the 1940's. We bend to authority because we are taught to. Just 80 years ago that mentality caused millions of humans to suffer and die because of their lineage. The only light found in that time were non conformist.

One of the ways that our culture contributes to the quality of our lives every day without our realizing it is with the language that we use, and the way we articulate our ability to navigate this human experience. Humans are limited by what they can express, which is often why revolution is first ignited within art. When words fall short, other senses can pick up the slack.

By way of comparison, the English language is quite limiting in its ability to express complex ideas. It can be a useful thought experiment to think about some of the elements that have arisen out of our culture and to wonder how our language has essentially ensured that those elements are the only logical conclusion. For example, one limitation of the English language is our use of the word "love." We love our spouse, our best friend, our new car, and our favorite television show with all the same word. But love is far too nuanced and deep to be expressed with only a single word. There is love which serves as the ultimate reality. (In most religions, love is a synonym for God, whether the disciples of that religion are aware of it or not.) Love is the thing for most of us that actually makes life worth living. The feeling of falling in love is exhilarating and scary as hell, but there's truly nothing like it. The feeling of falling out of love or experiencing unreciprocated love can make it feel as if your entire world is actually collapsing around you, and nothing could be worth that amount of heartache, except of course the one reason that we continue to engage with the world in this way which is, to fall in love in the first place.

This limited capacity to articulate the different facets of love limits our capacity to understand it fully. It causes us to objectify it and turn it into a commodity such as we see on the hit TV shows *The Bachelor* and *The Bachelorette*. These shows are broadcast to millions of people worldwide. Since western culture leads the charge for most of the world, that same show is being replicated across cultures across the world. So, what is the point? Our language has funneled us into a misguided understanding of love. Just like with anything, a view that is too simplistic leads us to engage with it improperly. We treat it as if it is something to be won. We propagate that message to impressionable girls and boys all over the world through media and then we wonder why so many of us absolutely screw up the role that love plays in our lives and further, why that role is contributing to so much unhappiness. When you take something like the ultimate reality, the thing that makes life worth living in the first place, and then you turn it into a game which requires contestants to change who they are and to compete in order to win it, you can see why it is so necessary to question the things we believe and the things we are led to believe. The millions of viewers are humans that have families, kids, and roles within society. This is only one minor way that our language affects our culture in a negative way. If it limits something as big and as sublime as love, how else might it be contributing to our lack of connection with ourselves and our lives?

Few of us even love the activities that fill up our lives. As a social experiment, I asked just over 1000 people what activities in their life makes them come alive. Fewer than 100 individuals were able to give me a sure answer. Most people needed a bit more time to think about it. Shouldn't the thing that makes life worth living not be limited to our relationships with other people? Don't we have a right to pursue activities that inspire us? Don't we have a right to the activities that breathe life into our days? Shouldn't the thing that makes life worth living permeate every facet of who we are? Except that's not at all the tact that we take. We instead devise lists of things we should do, things that will make us acceptable to others, and things that will keep us safe from too much criticism or discomfort. Many of these actions are the only logical conclusion of the words that we use to describe them. By figuring out what we really value (or what we really love), we are effectively putting in place a self-selecting system for our lives. Things that do not resonate with us fall away, and it becomes much easier to say yes or no to different opportunities. We don't have to spend nearly as much time deliberating between decisions because they become clearer when they are weighed against what we value. Unfortunately, most of us are so unaware of our own value system that we act against it quite frequently. This is why passion and love should play a much bigger role in our lives. The apathy that currently permeates our lives is doing little for the expression of our souls. When you are operating with something as boundless as the soul, the least you can do is give it more words to express itself.

Since we are in many ways at odds or at a minimum, not aligned with the way we articulate the things that happen in our lives and what we are actually feeling, we simply won't gain this ability overnight. Just because today you decide that you are going to live out more of your values doesn't mean that the world around you isn't eager to stick you back into the box that it has fabricated. Just like your programming, you've spent an immense amount of time living a certain way. You can't reprogram yourself in a day. It takes constant awareness around what you are doing, the words that you are using, and every action that you are taking which is contributing to who you are becoming. It is worth pointing out here that research has also clearly shown that when you are operating from a place of alignment with your values, and you have clarity around not only what you are doing but why you are doing it, your ability to focus on that task and perform at a higher level is increased. Cultivating an authentic life born out of what we love is the most efficient way to increase performance. How many of us spend our time looking for the next tool, trick, or hack to make our performance better? It appears that if you spend time on the front end ensuring that you are giving a majority of your time to things that you value, a higher performance, not to mention contentment around that performance, is an inevitable byproduct.

Just like my empirical poll suggested, we don't spend time doing things we love because we don't know what it is that we do love. To make matters worse, we are never taught how to go about thinking about what we love and even if we were, we have a language that makes it hard to express it properly in the first place. Often, what's not working for you is simultaneously not working for other people as well. We just have a difficult time of labeling it or understanding why because we are limited by the culture from which we are produced. It is difficult to tell whether you have a real problem, or you are simply bound by the constraints of the language you are using to solve the problem. For most of us, the difference between a life we love and a life we tolerate is found once we become mindful of what's causing our dissonance. In many cases, it's the way we are defining love in the first place. We often can't remove ourselves from our environment enough to realize that we are too constrained in our set of solutions to find something that works for us. Our culture is funneling us into a certain mode of being and reinforcing that way of being through pop culture and mainstream education.

The narrative around how best to spend our money is certainly no exception to this. From the priority placed on the American dream, to the constant influx of marketing we receive, it all plays a role. The aim of this chapter is to make sure that the role it plays doesn't denigrate the quality of your life. We mustn't forget that the way we are living now is relatively new and more of an experiment than it is the norm. We are experiencing a boom in consumption that previously never existed. If you find that the new materialist perspective and all of its nuances aren't working for your life, keep in mind that you don't have to participate in the obvious way.

> "The average American makes $74,600 per year. The two largest chunks of the average American budget comes from housing and transportation. ($18,186 and $9,049 respectively.)"
>
> - 2018, U.S. census data

Given my current age, my past income, and my net worth, I estimate that I have spent roughly $1,150,000 in my lifetime. If I look at every trip I've ever been on, every gym membership I've ever had, every road trip I've spontaneously embarked upon, every ski trip etc.....from that roughly $1.1 million dollars, I have spent at most, $180,000 on experiences or things that I have done. The reason that is important is because if I look back and inventory my life, just about every single moment that I can actually remember was due to one of those experiences. For those of you keeping track, that is one hundred percent of worthwhile memories I've had, coming from less than sixteen percent of the money I've made. To put it differently, I have spent roughly eighty-six percent of my money on things that don't matter and that I'll never remember.

The truth is that the main narrative in our society is driven by genius marketers that would have you believe that buying something is actually akin to doing something. Think back to all the commercials that you have seen. Every single one is an empty promise of an experience that you most likely won't have, and if you do, certainly won't be solely because of your purchase. Cue the extremely effective Nissan Xterra commercials. Did anyone actually believe they would live a life of adventure because they bought a $34,000 SUV with a built in $40 first aid kit? On some level they certainly did, albeit a subconscious one. The best adventures that I've had personally were all derived while on foot. The car that I drove to the trail-head was irrelevant. Our society encourages consumption and like anyone who has tried to kick an addiction knows, overcoming that is actually a lot more difficult than you might think. You have to consciously pay attention to your decisions and what is driving them. More importantly, as stated earlier, you have to find an even more productive replacement for your time once it is no longer filled with empty promises. This consumerism is actually just an extension of our perpetual desire for something beyond ourselves to make us feel whole. As you walk around the store for example, what you see is a thousand taglines that promise you a feeling. What they don't tell you is that the feeling is derived from your brain chemistry in a way that's going to leave you wanting more.

Ask yourself if what you are doing now and what you are about to finance will matter if you are lucky enough at the end to reflect and look back at your life. Like it or not, we have a finite amount of time attached to our lives, so you should think seriously about how yours is spent. One of the biggest tragedies of all time resides in the fact that we push people to trade their time for dollars and then push them further to trade those dollars for things instead of a better time. I find it difficult to see the nobility in the rat race when that is the outcome.

Perhaps it's time to start moving the needle in a meaningful direction and rerouting funds toward a life that matters. Although some of our spending is inevitable (food, shelter, clothing), I have found it better to minimize those things as they won't matter in ten years anyway. What will matter is the trip that you take across the country for a girl or guy you think that you may have chemistry with, the nights you never slept contemplating life with a friend, or the donation of your time or money that you made to help someone else's rough times get just a little bit easier. All of these provide a chemical release known as serotonin, which is linked to long term happiness and satisfaction. Compare that with retail therapy which provides a short hit of the neurotransmitter we've already explored known as dopamine. Dopamine gives you momentary happiness and as many of us have found out the hard way, some sort of buyer's remorse often follows it. This system works because by the time you get stuck with the bill after the "feel good" chemicals have subsided, there will be a thousand other things for you to sink your hope into that promises a return of that feeling.

The truth is that each of us were born to contend with the unknown and the wild, and our brain chemistry supports that never ending evolution. An unexpected side effect of consumerism is found in the fact that you can now recreate the chemical reaction on demand. The same type of feelings you get when you are pushing into the unknown are now found in things that will keep you profoundly stuck. Not only will you not be pushing into the unknown, evolving yourself, and your character, but you are likely to find yourself not doing much of anything at all. The truth is that humans were meant to not only face the unknown, but to stand in it. Humans spend their lives seeking the constant balance that allows them to flow freely between the routines and habits of their constructed world, and the evolution that is often forged on the frontiers of that world. This mode of being isn't only driven by the heart as you see with excessive dreamers or spiritual seekers. Each of us is internally wired to tame the chaos and live with the constant hunger to do so.

The truth is that we haven't been around very long and we are still evolving at an expansive rate. We are just far too close to ourselves to see how any of our newest lifestyle modifications will play out in the long term. Eventually, the masses will become aware of the best way to integrate the synthetic and real, but we may have to go through a few generations of people handling it poorly. I would imagine that the people who discovered fire weren't expert cooks right away. The same thing goes with new tech such as social media and consumerisms.

It often takes multiple generations to see how something will truly play out. To revisit an earlier example, if you were born in Germany is

1930, by the time you hit high school, you would most likely feel as if the world was going to hell in a handbasket. The closer to Nazi hell you became, the harder it would be to pull your perspective away and realize you were living through just a wrinkle in time and that's concerning one of the greatest atrocities in recorded history. What you want to remember is that evolution doesn't move backwards. Progress, truth, love, and light always prevail. If they haven't, then you are in the part of the story where they haven't yet. No more. This is relevant now because I am extremely optimistic about where we are headed. My current sentiment may seem hypercritical of our current culture but it's only because I know we can do better. Our innate narcissism was ignited with consumerism, and then social media threw fuel on the fire. With every day that goes by, however, we are awakening to the fact that there is a better way to be. The pendulum always swings back.

We won't always believe that bigger is better, more is better and better is… just better. Eventually, enough of us will challenge that line of thinking and things will settle into a better balance. What if you were to take a moment amidst the chaos of no money down financing, money back guarantees, and holiday sales, and just ask yourself how your life might actually BE better? What do you need beyond what people tell you that you need? That's where your focus and effort will reward you with contentment and wellbeing. What might you be free to pursue or try if you decided that the dream of western culture concerning ownership didn't necessarily match your own? When you add up the cost of the typical "American dream" you're most likely looking at going into debt for both college and then a mortgage. Between the two, you have an obligated payment for the next thirty years, typically to the tune of a quarter of a million dollars or more. With that type of commitment, what kind of options do have if you want to pivot in your career, start that dream business, or travel to the place that you've always wanted to? Of course, you always have the option to live differently, but your freedom certainly won't be aided by the world of consumerism. At a minimum, perhaps a better question might be, "What if you prioritized the destination over the vehicle that got you there?"

We grip tightly to our things and our ideas believing that letting them go somehow correlates to letting part of ourselves go. What we often fail to understand is that this is exactly what is happening, only it should be celebrated instead of resisted. We are letting go of the smallest parts of ourselves. The parts that subconsciously believe we should place our hope in material only to realize over and over again that the hope is not lasting. Usually our temporary uptick in happiness fades long before the new car smell. What we are left with is a payment obligation and a lifestyle promise that was never kept. Your human experience will be maximized if you shove back against what tries to dictate your behavior. You don't have to have an appetite for rebellion, just a strong desire to live more fully and to feel more deeply. Spend your money on the things that actually make you feel alive. Whatever that might be for you in particular, you can rest assured that it will inevitably be where desperation, disconnection, and dissonance cease to exist.

Chapter 14

CHANGE THE WORLD, STARTING WITH COFFEE

"The purpose of life is not to be happy. It is to
be useful, to be honorable, to be compassionate,
to have it make some difference that you have
lived and lived well."

— Ralph Waldo Emerson

What is made of earth and exists on earth finds itself operating within the confines of gravitational law and physics. Everything that objects to gravity must be supported by strength until it reaches its final resting place, that is, the earth from which it came. The beauty of the human is that in our own way, we transcend this law. While our body is still engaged in the never-ending tug-of-war with gravity, our minds are prime to take flight. We can dream of and conceive massive undertakings and fantasy that allow us to find ourselves in union with things that are far larger than ourselves.

This is one of the pulls toward charitable work that we all feel. While by ourselves we are still obedient to the limits of an individual, when we take part in something such as a charitable endeavors that brings multiple people together, we find that we have the ability to create massive change.

The limits to cooperation cease to exist the more in tune with each other that we become.

While it's quite clear that we evolved for tribalism (we are safer, more efficient and far more competent in groups of people), it is also clear that this tribalism has left us wired for servitude. In many ways, our modern societies are just an extension of that tribalism mentality. If I hunt and you gather, then tonight we are going to have a far better dinner than if we go it alone. The same "feel good" chemicals, such as serotonin that we discussed in the previous chapter, are also released when you do something good for someone else. You are motivated toward it and rewarded when it happens.

It's also quite clear that as humans we have a deep desire to matter. We want to mean something, and we want that meaning validated by others. All of this forms an evolutionary cocktail that leaves us with a psyche that dreams of changing the world. This is turn contributes toward the evolution of the collective. When one person takes on poverty, we all benefit by living in a world where people are able to shift their brain capacity from worrying about meeting basic needs to worrying about how they also want to contribute. While not everyone takes this path with their newfound freedom and education, the makeup of the human psyche ensures that most do. Overtime, almost all will, as a life centered on self eventually leaves us with a deep wanting for more. This is also why the only direction that evolution actually travels is forward. Any time that it seems to be regressing is actually more of an exception than a rule. Fundamentally, we are here in the world to change it.

Where exactly does one begin when trying to change the world? Regardless of how altruistic your intentions, the complex nature of this task is so great that it keeps most people at a loss in how to try. Like anything complex, however, there is always a way to break it down to its simplest form. If a journey of a thousand miles begins with a single step, perhaps a better question might be, "How does one begin to change her own world?" If you can identify the first step, maybe you can ensure that you are at least moving in the right direction.

I once listened to a speaker as part of a personal development course I had attended, we'll call him Jack, explain to us that every morning he would buy coffee for the person that was behind him in line at the coffee shop. I listened as he told me of all the transformative things that had happened in his life due to this seemingly simple task. Apparently, Jack went to the bank at the beginning of each month where he would give them $50 and asked for twenty-five, two dollar bills in exchange. At least five days per week while buying coffee, he would hand the cashier a two dollar bill and ask that she apply it to the bill of the person who came behind him in line. Never waiting around for impact, Jack would take his coffee and just leave, knowing that "at least I started the day off doing something good," as he put it.

I listened as Jack recounted the people that had chased him down, mostly out of curiosity to talk to him afterward. He mentioned a few of the business deals that transpired from the interactions over the years, but mostly he just talked about how good it seemed to make him feel. As far as things you'll never regret, doing something for someone else every day, regardless of what came of it, will never make that list.

Michael Norton in his *TEDx talk*, "How to Buy Happiness," recounts an experiment that he ran in Vancouver, British Columbia. He essentially asked random strangers how happy they were. The ones that agreed to participate in the experiment were handed money as well as a note inside of an envelope. The strangers were then broken into two groups, based on which note that they had received. Half of the notes said, "By 5pm today, spend this money on yourself," and then went on to list some ideas for the spending. Among them were bills, expenses, gift for self, etc....

The second group had a note in their envelope that said, "By 5pm today, spend this money on somebody else." The examples given were a charitable donation, or a gift for others. The actual amount of money was random, some received five dollars, and others received twenty dollars. Later that night, the researchers called the people who received the money and asked them what they spent the money on, and how happy they felt as a result.

The people spent the money on an array of different things. The personal spenders reported everything from earrings, makeup, and of course, coffee. The group who was instructed to spend it on someone else had almost a different list entirely. Everything ranging from a teddy bear for a niece, giving it to a homeless person, or wait for it… coffee as well. Starbucks was actually the only group that had reportedly made it into both groups of people. The interesting conclusion of the experiment, based on the reaction of the people who were given the money, is that the people who bought other people coffee, legitimately reported to be happier, while those that bought it only for themselves reported being no happier at all. What's even more relevant is that the amount of money didn't make any noticeable difference. The only uptick reported in happiness had to do with whether or not they spent the money on themselves or someone else.

In 2016, the Huffington Post ran a survey asking their readers, "If you could say in one word what you want more of in life, what would that be?" The overwhelming majority of responses replied that they want more happiness. Turns out, the answer is only about fifty dollars per month away. The problem is that most of us are waiting for something. We are waiting for someone to come to deliver us from our pain, or waiting for someone to give us the raise that will bring the happiness we seek. Happiness studies are consistently showing that it is something you can create within your life, regardless of limitations. The thing to understand here is that happiness is often created as a result of how you interact with the people that are around you. If you are unhappy and still drinking coffee every morning, then your first step is apparent. You simply weren't given what you have to hoard it. The universe is abundant, but it won't feel like it if you aren't.

You are always creating the world you live in with your thoughts, actions, and speech. If you spend your time creating happiness for others, the benefit is that you get to live in a world where others are happier. If we take into account the fact that as humans we are wired for servitude, this conclusion makes perfect sense. Nowadays, we are all trying so hard to get somewhere and to be someone that we've essentially gotten lost along the way. Our drive has put us in a position where we prioritize the wrong aspects of life. We have put far too much stock in things that do not matter. Things like social media validation or whether or not we are living up to arbitrary standards instead of our own.

Happiness, of course, has no substantial metrics outside of subjective thought. As a result of our need to climb societal hierarchy, we tend to forgo happiness in search of things for which we can measure and receive validation. One of those things that has become prevalent in our lives as of late are "likes" on the various social media platforms. We are addicted to the dopamine that we receive when someone "likes" a picture or post on social media. Again, we find that we are synthetically recreating what we were meant for, and getting lost as we try to navigate it. What's worse is that new media companies have become well aware of this fact. In order to keep you hooked, they essentially engineer the algorithms to keep you on a steady drip of dopamine after you post something.

They will first ensure you get a lot of likes (relative to your following) up front, but then they will continue to show that post to your followers at periodic times throughout the next few days so that you receive a constant drip of dopamine -- just enough to keep coming back and refreshing your feed. They monetize your attention by hijacking your brain chemistry and trading your contentment for their bottom line. You don't have to reject such a thing, only keep it in mind so that it doesn't control the way that you feel about your life. There is no amount of validation that can actually prove to be worth feeling poorly about in the short period of time that you get to be here.

This calls into question the distinction that must be made between pleasure and happiness. Pleasure feels great, but it will feel less great over time. Over more time, the dopamine in these activities will see that you are pushing harder for less and less of that original feeling. We want to slay dragons with this lifetime, not chase them. In his book *The Hacking of the American Mind*, Dr. Robert H. Lustig wrote, "Corporate America has been selling us pleasure disguised as happiness for some time now — think

Happy Meals, happy hour, and the smiling emojis we use to tell our friends we like what they do."

As we seek pleasure, we are seeking happiness in the most selfish way possible. The result is that we are constantly struck by anxiety (the worry of what could happen to us is a natural byproduct of all of the attention we put on ourselves). It also means that we are becoming less connected to those around us. Every day, we stand in lines with other humans at places like Starbucks, but we prioritize the dopamine from the screen over the serotonin that we could have if we engaged with those other humans. The entire time we are staring at our phones, the person behind us in line is wondering how they are going to tell their boyfriend or girlfriend that they are pregnant, or wondering why no one likes them, or why no one has liked their Instagram post as they incessantly refresh and stare away at their own phone. The entire time, you could have parted with an extra two dollars and helped begin to turn the entire situation around, for both you and them.

Chapter 15

THE PRICE OF SETTLING

"Don't ask what the world needs. Ask what makes you come alive, and go do it. Because what the world needs is people who have come alive."

— Howard Thurman

It's normal to feel as though you want something, but that the thing that you want is at odds with what you believe that you can have. The resulting life is stuck somewhere in the middle of beating yourself up for wanting it or for trying to get it. The real issue is that most people are not at all comfortable questioning their internal belief system, and instead will wrestle their entire lives with what they want. Before they ever get it, they believe it will always be there to remind them that they can't have it. I am betting that if you were given a magic wand, and told that a single wave would render your entire life perfectly as you would want it, you would find that you are not currently living that dream life. You may even think that's obvious because you would want a million dollars, or a mansion, or a sports car, or some other arbitrary metric of success that you've overheard other people are talking about, but that vision is just a stand in. What happens is that people have formed ideas about success throughout their lives and until they really let themselves go for it; they will keep that picture of what success would look like. That's usually how they would answer, "If I had a million dollars." If they never let themselves pursue or attain that dream, it will be the thing that remains in the distance and stands as the symbol of what they can't have in life. Often they will reason that it's not for them, and the advice they will give others is that, "You've got to be reasonable." Those are the most common type in society today. The ones who went out on a single limb, had it break, came back, and concluded that it wasn't reasonable to ever stand on a limb.

The next common type are the ones that really let themselves go for that first version of what success looks like to them regardless of the pain it incurs. This often results in an eventual extreme shift in worldview as they get close enough to the glitter to see that it's not gold. It doesn't matter if this person built a million dollar business, a small business, or become a nurse or anything else. What happens is that they are making judgements about success and as they succeed, they tend to realize that it's outside of their value system. Usually it's around three or four decades into life where people decide that they want something else for their lives than what they originally thought.

Sometimes family becomes more important and sometimes impact to the world becomes more important. In any case, this second group of people often get stuck feeling as though they can't pivot. It is as if there is too much pressure on them to maintain the kingdom and the appearance. Regardless of your formulated picture of success, what I want to bring to your attention is that it can be questioned. There are different roles for different people at different times in their lives. Your life isn't measured by the one game you were meant to play but by how you conduct yourself as you play many games across the span of your life.

While we tend to kick life off by using comparison to build our model of success in the world, that model should be up for questioning at any time. Consistently do your best to ask yourself the hard questions about what you want. As yourself if you are actually going to be happy. In fact, ask yourself if you would still want that thing if no one was ever going to know about it. That's where you'll be happiest. If we dug into those things and questioned them, you may find that they don't hold up to scrutiny. Why do you want those things? What do they really mean to you? What do they represent to you that makes you feel like you need them? What else do you want? What are your relationships like? What is your schedule like? Who are your friends and what are they like?

There are arguably many ways to go about getting your dream life, but all of them are useless if you don't know what that life looks like in the first place. Go beyond material and truly learn to build a vision for your life. What would your soul need? What would you need in order to wake up every single day and feel like you are living a life that is worth all of the struggle you put into it? This is a question that needs answering because lots of people are out here acting as if life isn't worth it. My question would be, "Have you ever given yourself what you really need?" Not what you want because that's subjected to material status and wounded behavior, but what you need? What do you need to feel centered? What makes you come alive and breathes life into your days?

We have to try not to let outside expectations box us into living smaller, and then resent the entire system when our lives are smaller or less than we want them to be. It's a form of victimizing yourself and it will happen to anyone that isn't aware and doesn't demand boundaries around their ambition and time here on earth.

If we got down to it, most people wouldn't even know what direction in which to wave the wand. This is because most of us, myself included, are somewhat lost to who we really are and what we really want. Much of that stems back to the fact that we are fighting a battle with the should mentality.

The advantage for that second group of people is that they have engaged with the world enough to see that everything you could want often turns out to be a false utopia. What they find out is that humans weren't meant for utopia. We need the right amount of trouble and hardship to forge ourselves against, and a full life won't be yours until you go out and learn what that hardship is trying to teach you. Often what we do want seems individualistic in nature, so we bury our true ambitions deep down inside. We are conditioned to believe we should want something more altruistic or more responsible than what we do want and so here we are, gridlocked in the middle, doing what we think we should do and avoiding what we want to do. You have to learn to reconcile your own intrinsic value system with the one the world put on you or you will spend much of your time in the fight that never lets you have what you want. We never face the things that we really want, so we set up shop in the land of "should," the land of settling and mediocrity. It's where we've built our entire culture. You do want money but believe that you should only want virtue, so deep down the confliction manifests as resentment -- resentment toward what you want, but what your subconscious won't ever allow you to have. *"Rich people are greedy anyway."*

You do want to look good naked, but that sounds vain and you should strive for health and self-love, and since you've decided those things are at odds, you relent and that manifests as baggy clothes hiding a body you'd rather not show off and ambitions you hope to keep hidden as well so that they don't earn you a label of "conceited." You think if you want to change something about yourself, you must not love yourself. *"People that want to change their bodies are unhappy anyway."* You do want freedom in your time to do activities, hobbies, and things that interest you, but you should work hard at a stable job so that manifests as you working forty or more hours a week for someone else's dream, while you continue to live for the weekends. *"But they've got great benefits!"*

You do want to travel the world, but you should get a mortgage because it's "such a great investment," and that manifests as at least a quarter of a million dollars in debt, handcuffs to the job you may or may not like, and a semi-permanent anchor ensuring that you never get to explore all of the areas in the world that are begging for your presence.

"But it's the American dream." You do want a relationship that gives you sex like a nineties R&B song, adventure you can't believe you get to share with anyone else, and a level of comfort that allows someone else to know you for your quirky, true self. But the last time you went for it, you got your heart broken and who in the hell would want to repeat that? Plus, according to society you should be settled down by now, so we stick with

the safe bet and all of our setting down inadvertently becomes settling for. *"But they're good to me. Plus, dating is hard."*

You want to be known for having done something great. You want to be known for having made a contribution to this world that you can be proud of. On some level, we all crave significance. But you have surely been told to be wary of taking on too much. And maybe that's true. Maybe the weight of your ambitions would crush you if you ever really went after them. But then again, maybe they wouldn't. Maybe you are actually perfectly positioned to accomplish that one thing you've always wanted to do, or running that one business you've always wanted to start. And isn't this inauthentic life kind of crushing you anyway? Sure, it's not an acute pain. But the constant vying for attention from people that don't freely give it and desperately trying to live up to someone else's invisible standard can't be that easy.

It's likely that at least one of these "shoulds" are running your life right now like they do mine when i'm not aware. We have a seriously hard time confronting the things that we really want because of some sort of misplaced altruism or allegiance to a standard we never asked for. Which calls into question a bigger problem. We are settling - but do we even know what the actual cost is, of all this settling? The cost is precisely what the outcome might be if you stopped settling. But it's actually more than you might imagine, because there is more than just you to consider. There is the personal cost which is essentially the life you are leaving on the table and won't get to live as a consequence. There is also the impact to the world at large. What if you began to prioritize yourself and the things that you want? How much better might your life be? How much happier might you be? If you were to be happier, fitter, or have more money, how much better would you be positioned to help the world around you? Think back to the previous chapter. How much better could you impact the world should the cost of an extra coffee have no bearing on your budget? What if your radical change in health inspired the people around you to do the same? Finally, what if you believed that a happier and healthier world started with you first giving those things to yourself?

If you were to tend to your needs first and foremost, and ensure that you were the best possible version of you that you could be, how much better would the world be for having someone as amazing as you in it? This is the paradox. This is not opposition. To help others we must first help ourselves. To love others, we must first love ourselves. We don't do these things for ourselves at the cost of others. What business isn't the world getting because you're too afraid to start it? How much better would that stranger's day be if you smiled in the morning because of the opportunity before you, instead of glumly walking by as you head for the fate you feel locked into? This is going to sound radical, but what if we all smiled in the morning because of that same opportunity? It's almost impossible to know the ripple effect that chasing our ambitions would have if we were to place them in the right place. What we do know for sure, is the outcome when we allow the fear of going against the grain to dictate our actions. This is worth noting because you're already aware of the downside. If you go for it, like really go all in on the life that you want, and it ends up not working out, you know you can go back to living for the weekends. The rat race is always accepting applications.

All of the things that you should do are zapping you of your energy and robbing you of your natural gifts and talents. The unfortunate by-product of that same settling is that the world is being robbed of the authentic you. And that "you" might be poised to do something great. The chances of getting your dream career, relationship, or lifestyle might be slim but they are not zero. Right now, while you cling to what appears safe and familiar, while you avoid your true ambitions like they're that weird guy you went on one awkward date with, they are zero. Quit being so afraid of what you really want. You want to have your cake and eat it too, but we have all been conditioned to believe that this isn't a realistic expectation. The truth is, having a cake you're not allowed to taste would suck. The same thing goes for your life. Figure out exactly what it is you want and begin baking. But don't think for a second that it won't take work. Metaphorically speaking, figuring out a way to eat cake and still look good naked is no easy task. The way I see it, we don't have an alternative. A life of constant safety is nothing more than a slow death. Don't you want the best for yourself? The best experiences, the best foods, and the best the world has to offer? Aren't you worthy of that? Aren't you going to be working hard either way? Aren't you going to struggle either way? We get what we accept in this life and if you accept a life that you should want, you'll never get what you actually want.

Make lists of things you want to do, places you want to go, and experiences you want to have. Explore things and ideas that interest you. For God's sake, make this life your own. Go out on a limb, ask that person out on a date, go against the grain, start a business, dedicate yourself to things even if other people don't understand them. Say yes when you are scared, and no when you are bored. Start practicing radical self-awareness. Do the world a favor and just be you. Unabridged, raw, original you. In a world full of half-hearted replicas, we could use more authentic humans. You might not create the next Apple or Google, but honestly, even waking up in the morning with the hope that you might is about a thousand times better than punching the clock, day in and day out, laying bricks for a building in which you don't even want to live.

Chapter 16

BUTTONS THAT MAKE US FEEL GOOD.

"Incredible change happens in your life when you decide to take control of what you do have power over instead of craving control over what you don't."

— Steve Maraboli

In order to fully understand yourself, what you truly need is objectivity. You need to step away from the emotions and try to understand yourself as if you were someone else. Observe your thoughts, your actions, and the things that you say. Look for patterns of behavior and feelings so that you can deduce the motives that inhabit you. You may find in doing this that you are clinging on to stories or narratives about yourself, others, or the world that simply aren't serving you. When you are clinging to a narrative with a strong emotional tie, you aren't free to full learn from it.

As it turns out, evolution has made doing this much more problematic than you might imagine. Here's why. The fact that you or I can judge ourselves at all gets us into what it really means to be human. We are aware that we are. Being self-aware can make living much more difficult. Namely, because we are aware of the fact that we are going to die, that we can fail at things along the way, and we can judge whether or not we acted rightly in any given situation. This "knowing" is our consciousness. The price we pay for knowing is anxiety. As we are aware of the world, we are simultaneously aware of the vast unknown elements that constantly surround us everyday. Anxiety is the result of you psyche contending with that unknown.

Coming to terms with the realities of our existence has caused us to evolve psychological coping mechanisms over time in order to dampen the blow that they have on our psyche. Our psyche is fragile but it knows how to protect itself. These coping mechanisms make objectively assessing yourself and how you are doing in any given task much more difficult than you might imagine. We essentially lie to ourselves to protect our own fragile ego and we do it often. Once we lie to ourselves, our brains are so incredibly good at confabulating supporting evidence that if we never stop to question it and try to create some objectivity, it's likely that we'll go on for years without a realistic view of ourselves or our behavior.

To add to the complexity of our situation, understand that when you are rationalizing your own behavior to yourself, your brain is doing so outside of your awareness. Without thinking twice, we tell ourselves that we are doing better than we actually are. Or, we will tell ourselves we are less capable than we actually are. In both cases, our mind will confabulate facts in order to back up its own theories. We often make things up such as these that act as barriers meant to keep us from reaching too far into the unknown. The problem is that all of these coping mechanisms make accurately gauging our lives extremely difficult.

We usually can't see through our own self deceit and so we just continue down the path. Nothing ever too wrong and nothing ever too right. When we get in the habit of lying to ourselves, the best thing that we can hope for is that we start feeling really disconnected from our own lives in a major way. This internal dissonance is often the error message that we need to start steering the ship in a different direction. Or to at least begin reassessing what we've already taken for granted.

Making assumptions about your emotional wellbeing without actually checking in on yourself is a breeding ground for quiet desperation. This is how the entire world ends up living in delusion about who they really are, and the position in life that they occupy. True self-awareness happens when you lift the blinders and stop lying to yourself. You simply cannot be delusional about who you are and still expect to act in the world with much success. You'll never get where you want to be if you don't know where you are starting from.

People are often content to live in this delusion because it feels safe to them. One of the things that happens to people when they start doing more emotional deep work, is that they are struck by deep feelings of overwhelm after they begin. Often what's happening here is that for the first time they are comprehending their own behavior and the mess feels like it's a lot to sort through. After getting a full view, people will pull the blinds back down and do their best to bury the discomfort but because awareness doesn't go backwards, they will eventually have to contend with the responsibility that's waiting. When we aren't self-aware and we are simply doing what we "should" do, or what we've been told to do, then it isn't our fault when things don't work out, or our life doesn't turn out to be as good as expected. Self-awareness brings with it the responsibility to act on our capabilities and facing our true potential tends to scare the living shit out of us. It shifts the onus onto us, and we realize that no one but us is responsible for the quality of our life.

You'll also have to work on overcoming the mind's affinity to take the path of least resistance. As you dive into your own inner game, it's possible that your subconscious mind will turn you away from going too deep. Often when you begin confronting the uncomfortable parts of your life, you'll find your subconscious has shifted your perspective to something else, something with less friction to ease the struggle. In writing this book, I personally find myself picking up my phone at random times to scroll mindlessly on social media. If I look back carefully, that happens every single time I am having trouble making sense of a topic or connecting dots in my mind. Your mind will choose apathy over struggle if you give it the chance.

The positive aspect of this self-awareness conundrum is that you will eventually learn enough to see that you don't really have the right to pass judgement over your life. Specifically, negative judgement. You simply don't know enough about yourself to know of what you might actually be capable. Since each of our potential is built upon what we do and not what we innately have, any kind of success in life is contingent on you putting your hat in the ring. It is not enough to simply sit back and assume anything about your own capabilities when you haven't: 1. Looked at your life objectively, and 2. Actually gotten in the arena with clear eyes and began to work. Reality rarely provides the feedback that we assumed it would.

One such area that we tend to walk around extremely misinformed about ourselves is in the type of control that we tend to exhibit over our own lives. We think we have control when we don't. We feel victimized when in fact we are the reason for our own suffering and perhaps the biggest transgression against our own well-being, we exhibit ownership over an outcome that we have no business trying to control. We need to become aware of how we do each of these things in our own lives so that we can learn to combat them. When the voice pops in your head and tells you that you aren't good enough for X, Y, or Z thing, or when you find yourself telling yourself not to pursue something out of fear of failure, it's important to realize that the voice is playing off of the uncontrollable factors in your life. You have no idea if you'll fail. You have no idea if you're good enough. There actually is no way of knowing without stepping into the unknown and so you find that you are in a trap. Only action will free you from it but by filling the unknown with negative situation that you are afraid to step into, you see stepping forward as impossible. This is the game that the inner tyrant plays to keep you small.

One of the ways that we can transcend this trap is by focusing on the controllable factors in our lives and building a case for ourselves. We need to empower the voice that knows that after you've done all that you can, there is nothing left to do but step forward. Sometimes when you get in an argument about something you are passionate, you will find that you are digging deep in your knowledge base to lay out the facts for why you are correct. We see this often in areas where there is a team aspect. We see it in politics and in professional sports. People will cite studies, pull out random facts and data points, and if all reason fails, they'll often bring in intangibles such as emotions, morals, and ethics in order to prove their case for why their team or candidate is superior.

Incredibly, we don't use that same vigor when laying out a case for ourselves. We'll try all of the performance hacks in the world before we try just believing in ourselves. At the end of the day, if we aren't our biggest supporters, who will be? Imagine a world where people build a case for themselves as much as they do for their favorite candidate or sports team. Instead, we tend to feel like we aren't capable of more than we are currently doing, so we pacify ourselves and place our hope and convictions in something outside of ourselves. Perhaps the candidate or the team that we've been defending. Again, I maintain the position that our lack of knowledge about ourselves doesn't give us the right to form an opinion about our ultimate potential. Chances are that you have drastically underestimated that which you are capable.

I say all of this as a matter of fact and not motivation. Until you do the work, you don't know enough about yourself to know what you can and can't do. In the end, if we want our lives to take on meaning, we must exhibit the proper amount of control over them. Taking control isn't about ownership over every aspect of our lives, but rather, having an accurate view over what we actually can control. Perhaps more importantly, it is letting go of what we can't control.

The nuances of the human psyche are consistently shown to influence our own behaviors in ways that we, the person experiencing the behavior, aren't aware. This fact continues to lay out a strong case for radical self-awareness, simply due to the fact that without such self-awareness, we will continue to live our lives at the mercy of feelings and emotions that we don't understand. When impulse guides our actions, it gives us the impression that we are a victim in our own lives, always subject to something beyond our control. For the tens of thousands of people that feel disconnected with their lives, much of that disconnection could be solved simply by giving ownership to the right areas of their lives and letting go of the wrong ones. In the end, our legacy on this earth and whether or not we are satisfied with our time here will be impacted by our ability to notice our implicit actions, and bring them into alignment with what we want and not what we've grown accustomed to accepting. This is the ultimate key to a good life but don't mistake its simplicity for ease of integration.

Your body and specifically your nervous system and your unconscious mind have trouble discerning a feeling from a thought versus a feeling from something you are actually experiencing in the world. This fact alone can have serious implications on the amount of dominion that you have over your own life. For example, if you are in a romantic relationship and you are constantly thinking about what might go wrong (perhaps you were cheated on in the past and can't stop dwelling on it), then your body is going to constantly "feel" as if that is happening now. It will be virtually impossible for you to be happy in that relationship as you contend with feelings of betrayal. This will only occur based on your thought of a past experience, and not on the reality that you are living in now. Subtle mental programming idiosyncrasies like this are consistently making us feel a certain type of way about what we are experiencing. It can be difficult to know whether that matches up to reality or whether we are just living out a narrative that we've already decided is correct. We often do this despite what reality presents us with.

The same can be said for any other facet of your life. If you think you aren't good enough to get a certain job or a certain amount of money, your body is going to feel that at a cellular level. How could what you want in the world possibly work out if deep down you already feel as though it hasn't? The reason so many people have trouble taking control of their own lives is because of the reality that is existing below the surface of their lives. You are a victim of yourself much more than you are any outside circumstances.

In psychological circles, the control over our own lives is known as having a sense of 'agency,' and it is highly correlated with an overall sense of well-being. Because we know just how deeply this sense of agency affects our overall well-being, it is something that we have to start taking more seriously. Often that means dissecting our own lives to see where we can exhibit agency and where we cannot. Commonly, people who can't seem to get out of the grip of difficult times find that it is because what they are trying to control is something that has already happened, or something that may never happen. In doing so, we squander what we actually have control over, which is only ourselves in this moment. The secret is that the moment is almost always perfect. We've just built a society that seems to have grown immune to it. We give our past permission to label us now and we allow the future to scare us from ever getting too far from the nest. When we continue to try and control what can't be controlled we keep ourselves in the problem that can't be solved.

It is also helpful to understand that our conscious experience in this world isn't a perfect representation of reality. It is subject to our own filters and because we know the flaws of our own filters we know that much of the way we experience the world is also flawed. For a simplistic view of how this flaw plays out, consider an observation by a sociologist in the 1960's, James Henslin. Henslin observed cab drivers in St. Louis who often played craps while in their downtime. Henslin observed that when the drivers needed a higher number, they tended to roll the dice harder and they were softer when they needed a lower number. Of course, how hard you throw the dice down has no bearing over the chances that any number will come up. Each of us do this throughout our own lives in subtle ways. We try to exhibit control because it makes us feel good. Many of us cling to irrational agency that doesn't exist for this reason. Thus, the case for objectivity if we want to actually increase our chances of positive results and experience instead of just feeling as though we have them.

Chances are that you do this quite often with a number of "placebo buttons" that have been placed in our everyday lives. The 'close door' button on an elevator doesn't actually do anything, yet you continue to press it whenever you get inside. The same thing goes for the button at most cross-walks despite the fact that the walk light is linked to the traffic patterns and has nothing to do with the actual button. The fact that there is no causal relationship between the action and the outcome doesn't seem to make a difference as long as people "feel" as though they are making a difference.

While this is easy to see with the use of "placebo buttons," I can't help but wonder where many of us are exhibiting this false sense of control in our own lives in many different ways. The detriment in this behavior isn't in pushing one of the many placebo buttons that surround us, the detriment lies in the internal narrative that ensues when we try to "control" something that isn't controllable. We evolved to feel good in the moment instead of seeking the truth but over time, the truth becomes required to feel good since what we want in life are actual results. Many people don't have a frame of reference for what they are doing wrong to cause their own discontentment because they have fabricated so much "truth" that its too far from reality to set them free.

This false sense of control tends to imply a narrative in your head. In short, if you believe that you are affecting the outcome when in fact it is random, then when the outcome is averse to what we want, the implication is that it is our fault. You see this in relationships when one partner chooses to leave another. If you've ever been left, you know how easy it is to blame yourself in this situation. Realistically, someone leaving is a reflection of them, what they value, and what they want. That's why we must only focus on how we show up in any given situation. Otherwise we end up carrying around a burden that isn't ours to carry. The same thing goes for the way that a parent might leave their children. That decision has been made independent of the departed, however the person that is left behind will continue to blame herself over and over and often this blame will end up shaping the things that person believes about herself. She might believe that she is unworthy or incapable of being loved when that has nothing to do with the true situation at hand.

The actual reality is that when a person decides to walk away from any relationship, whether it's a business dealing or a romantic relationship, that decision is squarely on the person leaving. Often times we might try to get leverage over another or to control them enough so that they don't leave but this stems from a false sense of agency. You have no control over what another person does. Instead our agency should be placed on ourselves. We can think about the kind of lover, partner or person that we want to be and then we can affect the way that we show up in the situations that call us to be that person. That is literally it. The rest is out of our control.

The truth is that you will never be able to be anything for anyone else that they can't be for themselves and vice versa. Your well-being is contingent on you understanding that. You must stop blaming yourself for situations that you never had control of in the first place. If time reflecting on a certain situation reveals that you wish you would have acted differently because different is truly what you wanted (as opposed to being different for someone else), then you have learned a lesson that is immensely valuable. You now know how to author your situations going forward and you have a standard for yourself. You just have to be careful that the standard that you have for yourself and your behavior is a true reflection of what you want and not what someone else might want. What someone else might or might not want is a moving target that you have no hope of ever hitting. When we influence the behavior over the part of the relationship that we do have control over (us) then we are doing all that we can.

Outside of our relationships, we tend to feel victimized by other aspects of our lives as well which often stems from being unaware of the level of control that we actually have. The jobs that we do, the place that we live and the amount of money we make are all usually a matter of our own control, yet these are the things that we tend to believe we are at the mercy of. Quite honestly, I am not sure what is more incredible. The fact that in the twenty-first century, humans have landed in a place where we have the ability to be, do, or have whatever it is that we might want, or the fact that most of us act as if that isn't true. We feel stuck in our situations in life and we self-impose a large amount of the rigidity around our lives that cage us in to a certain way of being. That cage is only opened when we direct our attention inward and realize that it is only ourselves that are holding the keys to the cage that we feel trapped in.

The truth is, you've already thought enough about what's transpired and what you could have done differently. You've already run through the scenarios about what might go wrong later. All that matters now is that you decide what you want going forward and then further decide to show up for yourself in this moment in that way. Whenever you find that you have fallen off the path a little bit, recognize that you were acting out of previous programming. If you want different, then you go back to showing up for yourself in the way that you want to. You don't chastise yourself because you weren't acting out of your conscious mind. In most cases, self-destructive behavior is wounded behavior. Just correct it when you notice it and move on. Over time, as you become less adversarial with your life and you become the one authoring the narratives that you live out, you will exhibit less and less of the behavior that you don't like.

The reality is that things are not always going to work out. Things are going to fall apart frequently because we're humans and we're clumsy, slow to learn and we prioritize how we feel over what we ultimately want. These are the things that teach us the lessons that we need to be who we are becoming. There are a great many more things that won't work out because of situations that are out of your control but this book isn't about them, it's about you.

Have you ever had a relationship end, romantic or otherwise, and instantly thought about all of the things that you could have done better? Often we will beat ourselves up about this whether it is true or not. We keep ourselves stuck in our own hell simply because we know we acted outside of our own values and the dissonance associated with that feeling is tearing us up. This brings the chapter full circle. You can't control what's happened, only get some objectivity to it, learn from it and apply those lessons to the one thing you get to control going forward. You. In this moment.

Chapter 17

LIFE IS MEASURED IN MOMENTS

"The heart surrenders everything to the moment.
The mind judges and holds back."

— Ram Dass

Before beginning work on this book, I had another one in mind. I set out
to write a book called *The Invictus Principle*. Invictus is often referred to as
the ability to master one's own fate, as described in the 1973 Ernest Henley
poem carrying the same title. My thought process behind the book was to
interview as many high performers as possible and tease out a formula that
you and I could apply to our own lives. Essentially, I wanted to create a
three- to five-step process that, if followed, would all but guarantee success
in your chosen pursuit. I wanted to know how we might learn to define our
own parameters for a successful life and what formula might help us
achieve it. This would be an easy-to-follow escape plan to avoid the drudg-
ery of an average life so many of us feel trapped inside of. I thought earnestly about how great it would feel to hand the keys to freedom over to all
the people who live lives of quiet desperation. Those of us who work our
tails off for thankless bosses while secretly craving a different life. A better
life. It had all the fixings of the next sexy self-help book ...and I was hope-
lessly naive.

Mathematical formulas work when there is only a single answer to be found. A + B = C makes sense when C represents a constant. An unchanging value with defined limits. If I were to tell you that hard work + an unlimited belief system = success, it would be misleading. There are other factors involved. Luck, timing, your support system, your daily habits -- not to mention the terms in which you define success in the first place. Even if all of those things could be accounted for, which they can't, we still have another problem. We are not putting this equation to paper in a controlled environment. The truth is that our lives are anything but constant and controlled. They are messy, dirty, difficult, chaotic, and they are filled with pain and struggle. They are also filled with inexplicable ecstasy and joy. They are filled with moments when you didn't know being alive could feel so good. It is those moments that make all the pain and struggle worth it in a way we can't always understand. You simply can't have one without the other, and that's what the human experience is: an unstable, impassioned paradox.

We're always living within an enigma of environments that are changing for reasons beyond our control, which induces feelings we don't understand. This, in turn, puts us in emotional states we don't or wouldn't necessarily choose to be in. Then we are left to pick up the pieces -- and that's what life is. You and I, up to our knees in mud, picking up the shattered pieces of what used to be, and trying our best to put them together in a way that will make something great. This is something worth looking at and talking about. We are always in flux, and if you can gain some perspective -- even in the midst of a storm -- the flux is what makes the whole thing so damn beautiful. It is knowing that although you're muddy and in pain, it's going to make one hell of a story when you're on the other end of it. It is also why there is no formula that works for everyone. We are dynamic beings that are complex beyond comprehension. That makes both simplicity and safety short-lived ideals within our lives. There is no path. There is no one size fits all approach.

Trying to look at our lives as constants that might be controlled and trying to define them within those limits will only lead to trouble. Yet how many of us do that? How many of us seek out the simple solution to a complex problem and then cling to it, hoping for a positive outcome? How many of us hold on tightly to what we know or what we've been told because it feels safe?

People make major life decisions about where to work, where to live and who to date based on what will lead to the most "stability" within their lives, failing to realize that any hint of stability is a false sense of security at best. At worst, it is the job that will never change deciding to let you go. It is the mortgage that will never decrease in value sinking with the market, and it's the spouse that you chose letting you down because we're humans and we do that to each other. The rug being torn out from under your feet is a lot more unsettling when you believe it can't be done. You are better off getting used to it, becoming friends with the change and the tension instead of fighting to resist it. The moments of tension are where life is lived. They pull at you in either direction, and you are perfectly capable of dancing with them as they do -- yet how many of us spend our lives trying to avoid tension in an attempt to get along? Often, we're fake in our inter-actions. We lie to each other and to ourselves because pleasantries are eas-ier to stomach than hard conversations. But hard conversations lead to long-term satisfaction. Pleasantries lead to resentment when real life is boiling below the surface.

The fact is that so much of what we do today is a subtle attempt to squeeze the life out of our moments. We set the temperatures in our house so they aren't too hot or too cold. We do the same with our showers. We cancel the day's activities in the event of inclement weather, preferring not to go outside in the harshness of the world. Feelings are easily hurt, so we protect our youth with safe spaces and trigger warnings. All of this despite the fact that a beautiful piece of art can never be appreciated if you never remove the bubble wrap. We answer questions about how we are doing with, "I'm fine" or "Good, but busy." We are taught to make our decisions based on what is safest and not what might yield the most growth. That begs the question: What are we here for? If we are here solely for safety and productivity, then perhaps we are on the right track. If we die and God commends us on our lives of stability, I think we have a lot to look forward to. We look for a heaven complete with soft edges, 401ks and conservative traffic laws. Nothing tempts me more than an eternity of "Good, but busy."

What if that's not why we're here at all? What if we are here to live not as we have been -- on perfectly paved roads with big buildings and even bigger egos -- but as something more, something deeper? What if the temperature was never regulated? What if we were never regulated? What if you found the highest possible ideal you could imagine, and then went after it with reckless abandon, all while acknowledging that the odds are definitely against you? What if the odds aren't important because regardless of your belief system, the odds that you are here now and that you have another chance to pursue something great means your existence has already overcome the most staggering odds imaginable? What if we're here to overload the senses with the best of the world instead of falling back to the same smell and feel of our old, safe habits? What if we're here to make the most of our physical bodies because our souls are infinite beings, desperately clawing to show the world -- and to show you -- what real endurance looks like? So many lives are faced with adversity; yet when tested, the energy contained in one human's willpower is so great that the only logical explanation is one of a soul that aspires to overcome. A soul that knows nothing of limitations and boundaries.

What if that's what you're working with? What if that quiet desperation you feel is the universe begging you to come play? To sleep under the stars or swim in the ocean, because this entire blue rock is a playground that's here just for you? To forget about what's safe in the hopes that you might find what's worthy? To be knee-deep in mud, picking up the pieces of your broken life, only to stumble upon someone else doing the same. And then to realize that your broken pieces aren't broken at all because they fit together perfectly. What if we're never actually broken? Just a puzzle piece that hasn't yet found their fitting.

Self-help gurus tell us we have to be positive despite our surroundings, but how do you stare out the window when it's raining and still manage to see the world for its beauty? You don't. Because denying the storm isn't living within the tension. You have to go out into it. You have to go to the beach and jump in the water while it's pouring. Then you'll understand that beauty isn't about aesthetics at all. It's about feeling.

Chapter 18

A BEARABLE DEATH
(THE CHAPTER ABOUT LIFE)

"Without birth and death, and without the perpetual transmutation of all the forms of life, the world would be static, rhythm-less, undancing, mummified."

— Alan Watts

There are numerous observable patterns about the human condition. Patterns which make it easy for us to speculate on the outcome of any given situation. Specifically, as we age, the ways in which the human body begins to fail has become predictable. In fact, there is no bigger data set than that of the eventual break down and deterioration of the human animal. If you subtract the roughly 7.4 billion people who are alive right now, the Earth has seen around 100.8 billion people die before us. Whether you like it or not, you and I will eventually be joining them.

Chances are that just in reading that you felt somewhat of a visceral negative reaction. Facing our own mortality is something western culture isn't great with. The conundrum of what happens next is a problem that religions, cults and prophets have been trying to solve as far back as history has been recorded. It is no wonder, facing the pasture beyond what we know and understand can be unnerving. I wonder though, what might our lives be like if we changed the phrasing of the question. Instead of wondering what the eventual cliff means for what happens next, maybe we should acknowledge that cliff and then ask, what happens now?

If this question isn't if we will die, the question then becomes, how might we live so fully alive that our inevitable death is rendered bearable? How might we make it so that our days are so full of life that by the time death touches our broad shoulders with its brittle hands, we have an eternal smile knowing that the world is unequivocally and unarguably better for having had us in it? That we didn't just leave our mark but did so on our own terms. That our presence was felt rippling through eternity on the back of all that we became in the time we were given.

This, as opposed to the heavy hand of death that grips and jars most of us toward the end of our days. Instead of a march toward the slaughter, might we run, swim, jump, lift, climb, dance and wave our hands definitely? Might our lives be a point of beauty that exists in rhythmic harmony with the surrounding world and might we recognize that beauty is exemplified due to its impermanence? Lastly, might we love in a way that transcends the impermanence of it all?

After all, that's what we all want right? To impact the world around us and the society that we've manufactured in some meaningful and lasting way? Isn't that why the last thing we do on Earth is etch our names in stone? A final plea for permanence? Could it be that our plea is misplaced? Despite our intuition we kick and claw to make this life worth it by material alone and although our grasping leaves our hands empty in life, we do the same in death. Even the headstones that we pay our last pennies for will eventually join the dust around them.

It is not simply enough for most of us to be perceived as having mattered, but to actually feel in our hearts and our minds like we are making a measurable difference. To love and be loved. To see and be seen. A statement that can only be made manifest by the way that you live -- the way that you show up now. If you forget about the impermanence of it all, it can be incredibly easy to trick yourself into thinking you have time to live this way later. After you've amassed enough.

We often spend our jobs working for the weekend, wishing our time away from Monday through Friday and then we tend to think we need more time to do what we want, become the person that we want and live the life that we want. What you actually need is to start living. You need to engage with more moments that make you lose track of time. It is ludicrous to spend your days wishing your time away and then to wish for more time. What you truly have is right now and when you act like it, you see that it becomes enough.

In many ways, the facade of achievement without substantial truth behind it leaves us feeling emptier than had we never done anything at all. It's as if the human soul has a deep seated desire to feel significant in a tangible way that can only be attained through intangible matters. When we give off the feeling of significance without actually having it, such as the way many of us appear on social media, the accompanying emptiness can be depressing. In many cases our temporary spike in dopamine from a flood of "likes" leaves us just as quickly as it came. It's as if despite the affirmation, we still have a desire to feel alive in the physical world. The one of which we were born and bred.

In short, we want to feel on some level that what we did with our time on this blue rock made some semblance of a difference to the others doing the same thing. We want to know that our vibration wasn't just lost in the ether but instead, echoed through the eons. That is an overwhelming thought. How do you leave your mark on something so vast in a way that anyone will see or notice? How do you do so when you have to pay bills, run errands and keep up with endless mundane responsibilities? How do you throw a rock into the ocean and try to compete with the waves?

I don't think you do. I think you figure out how to be fully present and relish the opportunity to be standing by the magnificence of the ocean at all. I think that's really all we have. We aren't here to compete with it. We're here to experience it all. Life reveals its mystery in the depth of experience, not thought. It is not enough to think about living while in an air conditioned room with clean hands. We must put into action the desire that's deep in our hearts.

You are just you and you get to experience the world in any way that you'd like to. To say that something as sublime as life needs to be validated by any other thing is a fool's error. It is this mentality that makes us feel as though the answers we need are somewhere out in the world. The world can guide you but the answers are within. You have to take a step back and appreciate your own life before you can ever hope to impact another's. To appreciate fully, you need to feel fully.

Maybe instead of avoiding the moments of discomfort, those are the times we should lean in. The moment we plunge into cold water, the nerves we feel before public speaking, the exhaustion we feel from staying up way too late connecting with someone on a level deeper than pleasantries -- we should pause and relish the discomfort because it's more than just discomfort. It's an indication that we're still alive and so for now, we're still in the fight. There is a moment when your body reacts to immersion in ice cold water. Your senses come alive in an effort to cope. Every cell in your body, which was lying dormant (maybe for years), is suddenly buzzing with vitality. Breath that you once took for granted is now choppy and shallow, as your lungs expand to their capacity in an attempt to inhale more oxygen. A heart that once beat automatically becomes elevated as it begins to shunt blood to your extremities in an effort to keep your core temperature warm. You will adjust and feel warmer after a minute or two but that's only if the water is still and you don't move around too much either. The second you shift your leg or move your arms, the thermo pockets against your skin will be disrupted and you'll feel the cold once again, clashing with the homeostatic temperature of your body. You might curse out loud, you might kick and fight to get out of the water but one thing you will know is that in that moment, you are indisputably alive.

Just because every minute brings us closer to the end doesn't mean that every breath isn't an opportunity for a moment to be savored in the meantime. Time passes but moments are etched into our soul in a significant way.

The way that we carry ourselves, the things we give our time and attention to and the way we live will say one of two things about our time here. We either happened to life or it happened to us. You will have spent your time on offense or defense. If the former is true, you stand a chance at doing the whole thing in a way that you are satisfied with. At the end of the day, that's all that I want for you. To fight every day so that when it's over, your legacy is one of advancement and defiance.

Your legacy in this life is a testament to the greatness that you leave behind in others. In this way, every moment serves as another chance to either increase impact and legacy or to accept what is as if you are serving a sentence. My hope is that whatever it is that you want in this life, you find it and that your passion for that thing burns so deeply that you are willing to die for its attainment. Passion that deep is the only thing with the power to inspire forward progress despite a known bitter end. Answering that call, despite those parameters, is the eternal call of the hero.

Regardless of what's transpired before now, you are reading this and so for now, you too are still in the fight for experience. You still have an opportunity to step into the hero role and do things differently.

You are a human and so some of your work here is accepting the fact that part of your story will be inconsequential in the long run. You have a body that billions of years from now will most likely exist as dust floating in the cosmos on a planet that used to hold life. You also have an operating system that allows you to reason with the gods and dream up the limits of your world beyond physics. You can lean into what doesn't matter and cite that as a reason to hold yourself back or you can decide that what's always been true is still true. You have this moment and this day and the hero is the one that steps up to face whatever it is that the moment holds, not because they desire the validation but because in all of existence, the opportunity to align yourself with what's right and what brings meaning is a gift that is uniquely human.

Between the cradle and the grave, a lot will transpire. Some of it will be awesome and the price we pay for that awe to occur is the opportunity for what's wrong to present itself. The human experience is one that sees us constantly navigating these polarities. At times we will use our head to navigate it all and the shadow of that is that what we think of as reason will make us feel pressured, shamed, limited and not good enough.

At other times, we will look into our heart for guidance. The shadow of that mode of being is that sometimes we will expose ourselves to being broken. If you feel that you've been broken, perhaps it is because it was time that you were opened and being broken open is the only damn way it ever would have happened. The answer in this case isn't to learn how to close yourself off again but to accept your invitation to live differently. Bravery in this life is measured in your willingness to show up to every moment fully open to receiving whatever happens. Sometimes what happens is good and in other cases, not so much.

What it means to be human is to lean into the activities, conversations and moments of discomfort because everything you do is a celebratory act of that very moment. It means that regardless of the setbacks and obstacles, you keep progressing, not because there is somewhere to get but because the best parts of this life reveal themselves in the steps we never thought we had the courage or talent to take. We were not meant for utopia, but instead, to shoulder the burden of never having it.

The greatness of a human is measured in their relationship with the unknown. Those who accept the lessons that it brings are given the gift of forward progress. Those who don't accept the lessons or try to keep themselves closed off from the experiences altogether find that life always appears to be closing in on them. For whatever this life might be for, one thing is certain and that's the fact that it rewards those who engage with it. It rewards those who set their sights on who they can become and over the course of time it tends to punish those who live for what they can do.

My hope is that you realize this before it is over. That way, whenever your internal energy is set free from the limits of your bodily structure, those whose lives were changed by you having been here can say that you did it right. That you lived in a way that rendered something as awful as death just a bit more bearable. That you stood while others knelt and set sail while others clung to the safety of the shore. That you were love amidst heartbreak, light amidst the dark, and music amidst silence. That despite the limited number of your days, you lived a dozen lifetimes, wrapped up into the one that you were given because you never saw an ending as the death of what was, but instead, the birth of what is and what will be. This is the eternal invitation to become the hero in your own life.

For continued work.

If you are interested in engaging more deeply with the ideas found in this book, I have created a course called the Clarity Academy, designed to help you apply many of these concepts to your own life. The course is a 12 week, online curriculum with the goal of helping you discover exactly who you are, what you want out of life, and how to think in order to make those two things possible. Check out that course and more of my content at my website: www.rickalexander.com As a special thank you for supporting my work, use code: Heroes at check out for 10% off.

Acknowledgments and sources used in the writing of this text.

Following what could only be described as my own 'rock-bottom moment' I felt lost, confused and burned out with my life. I found that I was constantly caught in the middle of what I wanted for my life and trying to be what I thought other people needed me to be. As I resolved to change my life and document the process through my writing, I began to find lights along my path that served to give me the direction that I needed. This book would not exist without those lights. Hell, there is a good chance that I wouldn't exist.

The people who wrote testimonials on the back cover of this book were integral to my healing and to the ideas that eventually found themselves in the finished product that you are holding in your hands. I have come to understand that the highest expression of our existence is found in the servitude of the people that we share this human experience with and I am humbled and grateful to be on the receiving end of that servitude and friendship.

In addition to my mentors and teachers, I would like to acknowledge Danielle McGinnis; my girlfriend, partner in crime and the greatest call to adventure that I've ever answered. I believe that in order for us to become who we are here to be, we have to have a worthy struggle to measure our-selves against. I have a million internal demons that would force me to play small in this life and keep me from being the person that she deserves, yet she gives me a door to a higher road. She gives me the opportunity to play the hero in my own life. In learning to be who I feel she deserves, I am invited to step up and face everything in my path that would stop me from being the hero. For that opportunity, I am eternally grateful.

Lastly, I know unequivocally that this book is only possible because i'm willing to stand on the shoulders of giants and pull from all of the wisdom that others have worked diligently for. In addition to the resources below, I found considerable inspiration from the work of the world renowned speaker and clinical psychologist Jordan Peterson, author and speaker, Rob Bell as well as the spiritual entertainer, Alan Watts.

Sources used:

1. https://www.psychologytoday.com/au/blog/supersurvivors/201805/the-paradoxical-secret-finding-meaning-in-life

2. http://www.swarthmore.edu/SocSci/bschwar1/SchwartzCulture.pdf

3. https://www.duq.edu/about/centers-and-institutes/center-for-teaching-excellence/teaching-and-learning-at-duquesne/pygmalion

4. https://variety.com/2018/tv/news/the-bachelor-season-22-finale-ratings-1202719232/

5. https://www.groundology.co.uk/about-grounding

6. Henslin J. M. (1967). Craps and Magic. Am. J. Sociol. 73 316–330. 10.1086/224479 [CrossRef] [Ref list]

7. McRaney D. (2013). You Can Beat Your Brain: How to Turn Your Enemies Into Friends, How to Make Better Decisions, and Other Ways to Be Less Dumb. London: Oneworld Publications. [Ref list]

8. Jordan Peterson, Slaying the dragon of chaos: https://www.youtube.com/watch?v=REjUkEj1O_0&t=1623s

9. https://robbell.podbean.com/

10. *Antifragile: Things That Gain From Disorder*, Author: Nassim Nicholas Taleb

11. *God: A Human History,* Author Reza Aslan

12. *The Hero with a Thousand Faces*, Author Joseph Campbell

13. *Man's Search for Meaning*, Author Victor Frankl

14. https://www.britannica.com/science/information-theory/Physiology

15. https://www.psychologytoday.com/us/blog/where-addiction-meets-your-brain/201404/your-lizard-brain

16. Shakespeare, William. The Tragedy of Hamlet, Prince of Denmark. New Folger's ed. New York: Washington Square Press/Pocket Books, 1992.

17. https://www.huffpost.com/entry/the-top-10-things-people-_2_b_9564982

18. *The Hacking of the American Mind*, Author Dr. Robert H. Lustig

19. https://www.ted.com/talks/michael_norton_how_to_buy_happiness?language=en